Grace
from
Head
to
Heart

Experiencing God's Kindness
in a Fallen World

Gordon C. Bals

Paperback ISBN: 978-0-9883283-2-7
ebook ISBN: 978-0-9883283-3-4

Library of Congress Control Number: 2021915856

Cover and interior designed by Jess LaGreca, Mayfly Design

Italics in Scripture quotations are the author's emphasis.

Unless otherwise indicated, Scripture quotations
are from *Holy Bible: New Living Translation* (NLT),
Wheaton, Illinois: Tyndale House Publishers. 2004.

Scripture quotations marked csb are from the *Christian Standard Bible*®,
copyright © 2017 by Holman Bible Publishers. Used by permission
Christian Standard Bible® and csb® are federally registered
trademarks of Holman Bible Publishers.

The Scripture quotation marked esv is from *The Holy Bible,
English Standard Version*®, copyright © 2001 by Crossway,
a publishing ministry of Good News Publishers.
Used by permission. All rights reserved.

The Scripture quotations marked msg is from
The Message: The Bible in Contemporary Language
by Eugene H. Peterson, published by NavPress, 2005.

Contents

Introduction

For all of us, certain moments in life mark or foster a significant personal change. Sometimes those moments are easy to notice, like a graduation. Or they occur subtly, like a passing comment from a friend that may come to mind after a period of time, as though lingering in the background of our thoughts.

One such moment took place for me in the spring of my senior year in high school. I'd received an appointment to the US Merchant Marine Academy, which was mentioned in our school newspaper. A friend chatted with me about that for a couple of minutes and, as he walked away, he warned, "I don't think you'll do as well there as you have in high school. It will be a lot harder."

My stomach tightened hearing his comment. But I quickly brushed it off, thinking, *I can work harder than anybody. I'll do whatever it takes to be successful.*

My goal in life was to become strong, independent, and self-sufficient. I grew up in a religious family, and we attended church, talked about God, and bowed our heads and prayed before we ate dinner, but I had not ever really considered depending on God, or needing anyone else. In fact I ran hard in the other direction. I don't remember feeling invited to become more vulnerable with or to trust God in more meaningful ways. Even if I had been invited, I couldn't have heard it. I had learned to distrust any close or intimate relationships. Some painful childhood experiences had strongly impressed upon me that I could not necessarily depend on others, that it was not safe to reveal vulnerability.

Whatever pain I experienced was buried under a mountain of achievement and self-protection. I was self-aware and hypersensitive; and in a world with ongoing opportunities for more pain and trouble, I became adept at avoiding it.

However, over the next four years, my friend's words haunted me as I met circumstances that caused my self-reliance to begin to crumble. So eventually during college, sensing that a better relationship with God must be possible, I tried to engage with God more closely, even though I wasn't actually seeking "intimacy" in any real sense.

I read Jesus's invitation to all those who are weary and burdened: "Take my yoke upon you . . . and you will find rest for your souls." (Matthew 11:29–30)

I definitely craved rest, but that invitation seemed strange to me. I had never admitted to being weary and burdened (that insight would take a while longer). Unknowingly, one way I avoided pain in those days was by gravitating toward Christian teachings and supposed biblical rules that seemed to reinforce, rather than disrupt, my self-reliance and self-protection. For instance, it was more likely that I would spend time memorizing Scripture than being out with friends. Religious duty hid my fear of relationships.

Much of what I did during that period took me further away from intimacy with God and any rest for my soul. At that point, my efforts to walk with God were actually making my life heavier, not lighter. However, to be fair, that's the way I thought it was supposed to be. A flourishing life was a reward for the diligent, the determined, the studious, and the hardworking—not for those who admit defeat.

What I learned about close relationships in my childhood was all I really had to bring to my relationship with God. In each of my closest relationships, I had to keep others at a self-protective distance, so I naturally did the same with God. As a result, my first decade of trying to develop any type of intimacy with God felt like running on a hamster wheel.

When the Apostle John wrote, "If we don't love people we can see, how can we love God, whom we cannot see?" (1 John 4:20), he was helping us recognize the profound links between our relationship with God and our relationships with others. Trying to get closer to God by performing for Him, becoming more religious, didn't get me anywhere. I was striving to become faithful enough, humble enough, penitent enough, and joyful enough to reach that rung on the ladder where God would look down at me and validate my belonging. I was laboring over this as though I were trying to earn a promotion, offering a performance for God to draw near to. I didn't open to Him the parts of myself that were lonely, broken, and ashamed—the inner person who was hungry to be known and embraced, but also terrified of that prospect.

So my life became full of religious activity—yet devoid of relational intimacy. I knew God's grace and goodness were real, but it seemed like those things must be for *other* people. I had a long way to go before I could experience more intimacy with God. I had internalized and covered over so much pain with self-protection in the past that receiving God's grace in the present was inordinately difficult. It didn't happen until I could acknowledge and accept the pain I had buried and tried to avoid. Slowly I began to recognize how pain in the present was an opportunity for me to recognize the ways I'd protected myself from pain in the past. I slowly became more aware of how I could be more vulnerable and trusting. Present-day afflictions tilled up the soil of a hardened heart and helped me practice becoming more intimate with God.

As I became more vulnerable and open with God, His grace began to penetrate my soul more and more. As soon as I admitted to God that I was weary and burdened, His yoke started to feel lighter and kinder. I stepped off the hamster wheel and finally began to experience rest for my soul.

The change was so significant that I became devoted to learning about how the trials of life could work on me and others in such a way that more intimacy with and dependency on God developed. In my master's and doctoral degrees, I set my heart on understanding the connections between our past and present pain, traumas, and vulnerabilities, and our relationship with our loving Creator.

As I began to counsel others in my work, I was increasingly drawn to work with those who had suffered tragedy and loss. Right along with those I counseled, I also learned more and more about how to become reconciled to God in a fallen, painful world. Over time, what I believed in my head (that God is infinitely graceful and kind) penetrated my soul and took up permanent residence in my heart.

My hope and prayer as you read these words is that you too will experience God's grace moving into your heart and nourishing your soul.

One

What Kind of Grace Are We Talking About?

*I*n order to grasp how grace moves into our heart, let's begin by addressing the type of grace we're talking about.

God is gracious toward us—he wants to show us favor and do what's best for us. We may often believe this in our mind without experiencing it in our heart. In some ways this is not surprising, because God's graciousness is so different from what we usually experience from day to day in our other relationships.

In Scripture we read, "A friend is always loyal, and a brother is born to help in time of need." (Proverbs 17:17)

In a world plagued with sin, suffering, and loss, we need good friends—those who are perfectly supportive and patient with us, and caring in our time of need. Such friends help us find the better parts of ourselves that we didn't even know we were looking for. They always seem to want the best for us, and willingly wait for us, while encouraging us forward in whatever way is helpful.

Not only are they constantly believing and nurturing the best parts of us, but such friends also grieve with us when we've fallen, and celebrate with us when we've succeeded. On top of that, if we hurt them, even as they feel the wound, they still move toward us with compassion.

You may already have that kind of good friend—but does anyone in your life come readily to mind who fits the above description exactly? That is a high bar to achieve.

That's one reason we may have a hard time relating to God as someone who never stops loving us like that. It can be difficult to trust God's grace, because others don't model it perfectly, and/or we have a heart hardened by pain that inhibits our ability to receive that grace. It can be so contrary to our everyday experience.

Life can be difficult and overwhelming, and it's hard to reach out for God's grace in all the circumstances we need it. And yet, we're needy! We cannot be, and do, all that life in this world requires of us without God. We need His grace every single day.

Thankfully, God is tender and compassionate, and He imparts all types of grace to those in need. For instance, many theologians refer to *common* grace that God showers on us, which includes all the undeserved blessings we receive from the hand of God—things such as rain and sunshine: "He gives his sunlight to both the evil and the good, and He sends rain on the just and the unjust alike." (Matthew 5:45)

Another type of grace is *provisional* grace. Through God's provisional grace, He meets more specific needs such as food, shelter, and clothing. As frail human beings, we cannot make it through life alone.

Sanctifying Grace

Instead of addressing common grace, or provisional grace, or any number of other varieties of grace that theologians have named to help us understand God's abundant love, I focus here on *sanctifying* grace—and specifically the way it comes to us in our most difficult moments. If we're sanctified, we become more like God, and we love as He loves. For this to happen, we must receive love from Him—and we experience this most poignantly in moments of pain or trouble.

The Apostle Paul articulated well the sanctifying process I have in mind: "God is our merciful Father and the source of all comfort. He comforts us in all our troubles so that we can comfort others. When they are troubled, we will be able to give them the same comfort God has given us." (2 Corinthians 1:3–4)

As we respond to God's grace in our difficulties, His love nourishes and strengthens us to extend that grace to others. In the middle of our troubles, when we might be wondering how much God loves us (because he hasn't rescued us from the pain)—these are the times when we need to respond the most to His help, but we don't really know how to respond. Those can be some of the hardest moments to receive His grace. We weren't originally made for a world with trouble; the Garden of Eden was perfect. So when we experience hard times, we often have a harder time being responsive to God's grace. It's what the ancient Greek dramatist Aeschylus referred to as God's "awful grace"—"Even in our sleep, pain which cannot forget falls upon the heart drop by drop, until—in our own despair, against our will—wisdom comes through the awful grace of God."

You can see reflections of this grace in the Apostle Paul's relationship with God. Like Paul, in moments of trial, we pray for God to remove the difficulty. (2 Corinthians 12:8) And of course, that prayer flows naturally out of any ailing believer. It's a good prayer. Often however—as with Paul—God doesn't remove the trouble; and instead He says, "My grace is all you need. My power works best in weakness." (12:9)

Our weakness is the prompt to stop depending on ourselves alone, and look for God's grace, which is always there. Moving toward God, instead of pulling away, helps us to find the better parts of ourselves.

Does it seem upside-down to take help in difficulty from someone (God) Who we know could prevent or take away our difficulty? But this is the crux of sanctifying grace. If we experience pain or tension in our relationship with someone, and don't know how to relate to them, we may withdraw from them or choose indifference. However, in those moments with God—if we open ourselves to His grace instead of reject-ing it—His grace will refresh and strengthen us.

Opening ourselves up to God like this doesn't require us to feign affec-tion for God that we do not feel, which is what some believers may do when affliction arouses painful or conflicted feelings toward God. If we've been taught to relate to God only in a "proper" way, we don't know how to relate to Him when we experience discomfort in our relationship to Him.

In those moments of trial, when God seems so absent or uncaring, it's hard to respond to Him and easy to move away from Him, and His grace. If we are taught to search and strive and push through difficulty using only our own strength, as I was for a long time, we can become hardened toward God rather than willingly relate to Him in our vulnerability.

He Is Looking for You

During painful times, we might feel like the Israelites, abandoned and weary in coming out of exile and moving through the wilderness, just wanting some rest. Here's how the prophet Jeremiah captured their experience: "They found grace out in the desert, these people who survived the killing. Israel, out looking for a place to rest, met God out looking for them!" (Jeremiah 31:2–3 msg)

That's the heart of sanctifying grace. During our weariness and unbelief, in a time and place where we need grace the most, God is out looking for us with the exact grace we need. At crucial times in the Christian life, the part of us that might naturally assume God is out looking for us may not awaken if the vulnerable part of us (that is thirsty for someone to help us) is buried deeply under shame, indifference, pressure to perform, and fear.

Relating through Uneasiness

We cannot be receptive to a God who's out looking for us if we don't have a framework or language that helps us become responsive to His grace during difficulties. When we feel lost, fearful, inadequate, or ashamed, it doesn't necessarily come naturally to respond to *anyone*, including God. Accepting our vulnerability in those moments is hard. Grace amid trial is hard to welcome and receive on a heart level. God is kind—but in a world filled with troubles and afflictions, this kindness can often be obscured and experienced only by those who live life counterintuitively—by considering the opposite of what we think is obvious. To do this, we must welcome the upside-down nature of God's enabling and restoring grace. And it's not always easy to fold into the grace I'm describing here.

Scores of books and articles and sermons teach us how to try harder to endure difficulty, or how to seek God when He seems distant. That is not what I'm talking about. I am talking about God's complete and enduring goodness to us, especially as we go through the hardships we don't handle well and want gone from our life—how He comes after us, helps us, and fights for our heart, despite our hopelessness and fear or our preconditioned determination to take on the fight all by ourselves.

This is what I mean by *sanctifying* grace.

I have not, in the purest sense, become more of an undivided, persevering believer during trial because of my own efforts or goodness. That has matured only through responsiveness to God's grace along the way, and with His help in doing it. I've become more responsive to God's grace in difficulty because He kept reminding me in trials—as I felt condemned, alone, or betrayed—that I didn't have to feel good about Him, and that the "awkward" God-consciousness I felt was a sweet aroma to Him. I kept awakening to His goodness amid trouble not because I was good, but because *He* was good.

The less I felt I needed to be "good," and the more I believed I could lean on His goodness, which I "didn't deserve," the more I responded to and was able to naturally accept His grace. To become receptive in trials—to have hope that the trials we face are not "pass" or "fail," and can help us mature and become more loving—isn't something we grow into easily or through focused effort.

Full disclosure: I still get lost in trials. However, my endurance has grown in a real way; and as I experience trials, I have more hope and assurance that God hasn't forgotten me. To get there, I keep accepting God's help and invite Him to perfect His life in me even as I struggle.

This is sanctifying grace.

Two

Opening Our Heart

I'll never forget the first time I heard a teacher explain the term "fallen world," which described how every aspect of creation was infected with distress and chaos after Adam and Eve's rebellion in the Garden of Eden. The teacher explained that we weren't "designed" to face the consequences of living alone in a fallen world. The three major things we encounter here—sin, suffering, and loss—are experiences we were not designed to confront by ourselves. Hurting others, being diagnosed with cancer, or waking up the morning after your child has died are not occurrences we're qualified to handle alone. Whether it's the guilt that comes with sin, the despair that accompanies suffering, or the anguish that follows loss, we all need help navigating those experiences.

It's impossible for any of us to avoid troubles, and we often forget how much courage, faith, and help it can take to navigate them in a fallen world. Some might naively think the world isn't really that painful until they hit that hard place. And for a time, some may self-righteously think, *I've overcome this world.* But what takes true courage is to be the person who feels the pain in this world and turns to the Lord for help.

As that teacher explained these things, it made sense to me and invited me to stop pretending that everything was okay. It also helped me recognize that I needed help—that I had closed and hidden my heart from God. So I speak from experience when I say that opening our heart in a fallen world is painful. It requires a vulnerability that we may truly want to avoid.

Every person has experienced the effects of living in a fallen world. Maybe you have watched a loved one succumb to a terminal illness, or you have worked for a boss who was a bully and regularly betrayed you. Or perhaps you do things that harm others that you don't really want to do, or take out your anger unfairly on another. We are all certainly familiar with some of the endless ways we encounter hardship in this world.

Troubles Awaken Us

Many people wonder why God allows us to experience such an abundance of ongoing troubles. And people have tried to answer this question from a philosophical or theological perspective through the ages. Many lectures, talks, and sermons cover the subject, and scores of books have been written about it. However, when God's Son experienced affliction, He didn't ask his Father a philosophical or theological question. He asked a personal question. On the cross, he lamented, "My God, my God, why have you abandoned Me?" (Matthew 27:46)

In *Disappointment with God*, Phillip Yancey writes, "If I ever wondered about the appropriate 'spiritual' response to pain and suffering, I can note how Jesus responded to his own: with fear and trembling, with loud cries and tears."

The pain Jesus experienced moved Him toward vulnerability with God. He modeled for us how to act when we experience affliction. We all face troubles in a fallen world, and those we love face them as well. We must learn to relate vulnerably to God in the midst of our suffering.

Jesus showed us a perfect example of how *we* need to relate to God when in the midst of trouble. We cannot approach God from a philosophical or theological posture in order to experience God's grace in our affliction.

It may not be easy to relate to God in the aftermath of difficulty; we may feel wounded by Him, or confused about His goodness. Surprisingly however, that wounding may be the exact opportunity to move toward deeper intimacy with Him. Trials often help us redirect our attention to God because we have faith in His goodness; and if something in our life isn't good, we may experience an aroused desire for Him. Over time, as afflictions bring to the surface our passion toward God, they help us express our hopes, fears, resentments, or wounds to Him.

The "answer" God gives us as we endure suffering may not seem rational, because His answer is simply *more of Himself.* The strengthening and hope we find that changes us as we engage God about our personal difficulties can become a profound clue to the mystery of anguish in this world.

I don't suggest this lightly. I don't suggest that God specifically orders tragedies to make us a better person. I also don't think we are ever to minimize the trauma anyone experiences by noting how some good can come from it. However, my experience has been that those who hurt honestly and passionately—and who retain connection with God through the process— become known by God and have more strength to love like Him in this world. As our afflictions often draw forth the ways we unknowingly hide from God or avoid Him, they also help us see our profound need for Him.

To be reconciled to God and become more like Him, we must relate to Him through the difficulties we experience. If we go through afflictions and harden our heart toward God, His grace remains only a concept in our mind. But if we relate to Him in a personal way, drawing near to Him while wrestling out our afflictions, grace moves into our heart.

An Example of Endurance

I now can see clearly that living and understanding this process has been my life's call. Whether it has been engaging God over my own troubles, studying the theme in a personal or academic way, or helping others in their afflictions, the topic has never been far from my heart. I've tried to hold the tension of faith and doubt, pain and beauty, life and death, in such a way that I—and those I care for—become more like Christ in this world. I believe God's "best answer" to the pain in this world is the love His followers demonstrate to counteract it. The world isn't saved by agonizing or strategizing over it; it's restored by people modeling the incarnational love of Jesus.

It has been an honor in my vocation to study, teach, and counsel others toward nurturing this kind of love amid the difficulties in this world. I've kept asking, "How do I become an answer to the pain in this world—and how do I care for others in a way that *we* become an answer to that pain?"

I can't make sense of this in a way that's rationally satisfying. However, finding kinship with others who endure troubles well, who stand against injustice that spreads affliction, and who live into the kingdom of God here on Earth, has helped me with the why of the difficulties we all experience. As we fight the tendency to let troubles bully us away from our desire to hold onto God and to love others, we connect with and share hope in the promise that our troubles will one day be no more.

I must stress that becoming someone who endures difficulty well is not easy, and it comes with a cost. It can be tempting to depend on ourselves to find ways to numb pain instead of going directly to God.

The particular season in my life when I realized afflictions in this world had restored me into a stronger, more-resilient human being is seared in my mind. I was enjoying a quiet ride home from work, imagining a relaxing evening with my family, when I was jostled from those serene thoughts by the ringing of my phone. I answered, and my oldest sister told me our mom had found a suicide note from our youngest brother, Justin, and that our middle brother was on his way over to look for him. The note Mom found was painfully sad, and ended with these words: "Sorry to disappoint everyone. I guess I was just bound to be a failure."

Those words could not have been any less true. Justin was a kind and thoughtful man who had so much good ahead of him. He was the youngest of my six siblings, born eleven years later than my youngest sister. He was born into a family with a preteen and five teenagers. All of us were transitioning from childhood innocence to adulthood. Justin was born into that mix and was the apple of all our eyes. He helped us carry some innocence with us into our adulthood.

So much of my adolescence was peppered with moments of connection and life with Justin. Two nights before I left for college, we went together to see the movie *E.T.* at the theater. On the way home, Justin—who was six at the time, began to cry. He said, "What am I going to do without you?"

As those thoughts were rolling around in my mind after my sister's call, I quickly got a second call. My brother had found Justin. He'd hung himself in our parents' garage—a beautiful life tragically stopped short.

I wept all the way home, and kept weeping as I climbed the stairs from the garage toward the kitchen. I couldn't quite make it. Several minutes later, my oldest daughter heard me in the stairwell and joined me. I told her what happened, and we cried together, waiting for the rest of our family to arrive home. I struggled through the next several days, continuing to weep off and on as we made the trek to New Jersey for his funeral. My brother's suicide brought so much to the surface about my past and the pain of living in a fallen world.

However, something stood out that surprised me. I wasn't overwhelmed by the loss, even though I felt consistent pain and heartache. I moved more restfully through that tragic event than I had through less-heartbreaking events in the past. I wasn't hardened to my feelings, swamped by them, or driven into a funk. My heart was open and regularly refreshed by God's grace, which helped me live more like Christ—hurting and loving at the same time. My family asked me to do the eulogy at Justin's funeral. It was hard beyond words. I simply wanted everyone to remember Justin's life, and what a beautiful man he was, and to grieve that he was gone. I wanted our hearts to be open to the nourishment we needed from God to endure his suicide. After the service, as we made our way out of the pews toward the back of the church, my dad—who's a man of few words in moments like that—said, "I've never seen so many people cry in our church. You lifted our family today, son."

Later in the week, my father's words caused me to reflect on other seasons when I'd faced hard or tragic moments. In those seasons I wasn't as alive and wouldn't have been able to offer a eulogy that was helpful to those in pain. I was too turned in on myself. In those seasons when my hardened heart was touched by afflictions, God's grace never penetrated. I was too self-protective to let the Lord or others in. However, as I grieved my brother's suicide, the free flow of God's grace strengthened my heart and helped me stay alive through the pain, open to God and others. That aliveness was experienced by others as I gave the eulogy at Justin's funeral.

Driving back to Alabama from the funeral, I thought about the weeks ahead, knowing they would be difficult. But I had no sense of dread. We got home on a Saturday night, and my good friend Mike made time to see me Sunday morning. We'd been in touch since my brother died, and he was helping me carry the weight of loss. He was one embodiment of

God's grace that sustained and refreshed me. His presence and life-giving words nourished my heart. We'd practiced for years at sharing each other's burdens, holding the hard and painful parts of each other's stories and celebrating the beautiful ones. So that Sunday morning, it came naturally. Several other friends offered similar support, and our family was well cared for through that time. My wife Dawn and our daughters Aimee, Abigail, and Elise grieved together with me, and we nourished each other's heart. We shared the loss as a family.

I returned to work after we got home from the funeral and was able to continue counseling other people who were hurting. I kept giving and receiving emotional and relational care during that time. In the most upsetting season of my life, despite the immense pain, I was surprised to find that agony and loss did not wilt the life in my heart and rule the day.

Endurance Is Not a Pass-or-Fail Test

The Apostle Peter wrote two letters to the persecuted Christians in the five regions of Asia Minor. Early in his first letter, he speaks of how enduring well through trials purifies our faith in the same way that "fire tests and purifies gold," though our faith is "far more precious than mere gold." (1 Peter 1:7)

When I first read Peter's words to believers who were being marginalized and slandered, it seemed cruel. Those reading his letters were struggling to own their faith. Later, Peter reminds them that "God opposes the proud but gives grace to the humble." (1 Peter 5:5)

Imagine hearing that advice as you're trying to hang on amid cultural pressure, and to believe God is for you? I would have preferred words like, "This has gone on long enough. God is going to vindicate you!" Or, "Don't worry, the persecution is about to stop." Instead, Peter encourages them to accept the way afflictions could soften their hearts by weakening their self-reliance.

That's hard advice. Peter doesn't tell them to be happy and buck up. He encourages them to bear up under the difficulty because it will reveal things they need to see about themselves that we often don't want to see.

In ancient times, gold was put in a clay vase and set in a fire to burn off dross or waste materials. The heat separated the impurities from the gold, and the craftsman stirred and skimmed the molten metal to remove any impurities that rose to the top. This is exactly how trials purify our faith. They help unseen impurities rise to the surface—impurities that stand between us and God's grace.

This process is also mentioned in Revelation 3. The Laodicean believers were "lukewarm" or ineffective. Their hearts weren't open and alive toward God. Their self-reliance kept their hearts closed. They thought they were "rich and didn't need anything," when in reality they were "wretched, pitiful, poor, blind, and naked." Their hearts were hardened and deceived, and they didn't even know it. To rectify their condition, Jesus tells them to buy "gold that has been refined by fire." In the process of that refining, they would become genuinely rich and receive white clothes "to cover their shameful nakedness."

The Laodiceans were lukewarm because they covered over their needs too quickly. When they were told to buy "gold that has been refined by fire," they were being encouraged to enter more meaningfully into the trials they encountered. Trials would open their hearts, expose their nakedness, and reveal their helplessness. Instead of turning into themselves, they could look to God and others and say, "Help me, I can't do it by myself."

Trials uncover the shameful parts of our heart that we hide, and we shouldn't quickly cover them back over. We're often unaware of how much we hide these parts of ourselves—and how much they're hidden from us. The Scriptures clearly teach that we're self-deceived; there are things about ourselves we don't know. Growing up as vulnerable children, we suppress or push away the shameful things we do or that are done to us. Then as adults, we're surprised at what surfaces as we face afflictions that bring to the surface what we've hidden from ourselves. As trials poke, pry, and uncover what we've concealed, they invite us to vulnerably open more of ourselves to God.

For me, it was a gradual process to welcome trials and let them till up the hardened soil in my heart. I now see that trials were not a pass-or-fail test, but the kind of test that revealed impurities so they could be sifted out. Trials wounded my self-reliance and invited me to look for help. As I let trials till up the soil of a protected heart, it helped me become more aware of—and responsive to—my need for grace. God's love and truth began moving from my head to my heart. Without trials, it seemed like I was managing just fine, but as trials awakened me from my naive self-reliance, my need for God's grace became more apparent.

The Fruit of Endurance

Becoming more aware of our need for grace is difficult. I'm sure you can remember encountering difficulties that you knew could be beneficial, but it was hard to walk through them that way. That's why it's important to remember that trials can foster an atmosphere where we find more of God's grace. They pry open places of pride and wounding, and invite us to receive nourishment from God. Although tender and raw, the vulnerable part of us that knows we cannot survive without God's grace is opened as we encounter trials. They tear off our scab of self-protection, and we become aware of lies we didn't even know we were believing, and needs we didn't even know we were hiding.

When I was a young believer, trials threw me off-kilter. Satan's consistent deception—that God didn't care about me and was holding out on me—became unavoidably loud in trials. I remember "June weekend" at the end of my freshman year in college. It was a festive time with many activities, including a formal military ball, and I'd invited a girl I was interested in up for the weekend. I liked her and wanted to get to know her better, so I was excited and nervous at the same time. As my date and I were driving out to the beach that weekend to spend the day together with friends, we got a flat tire. You may not consider that a trial. However, underneath my nervous joy was a foreboding that said joy was not for me. I was a young believer and convinced that what Satan regularly whispered in my ear was true. God was not only holding out on me—he was against me. In front of my date, I freaked out a little over that flat tire. Silently I started apologizing to God, begging Him to let me have a good weekend. (There were no future dates with her.)

At the time, I was so disconnected from God's grace that when any trial, small or large, entered my world, it was proof I needed to behave better, because God's grace was not for me. Whenever I encountered situations that brought my need for help to the surface, the drama in my mind intensified, pulling me toward the belief that I was alone, and God didn't care about me. The atmosphere around any trial I experienced pushed me into myself instead of toward God.

Nevertheless, God steadfastly and kindly pursued me, and I began to awaken to His grace in trials. I gained the ability to let afflictions uncover needy parts of my heart and help me practice at relating vulnerably with God. As I stopped turning into myself so reflexively and stayed open to God longer, I developed the capacity to welcome words and actions that soothed and healed a broken heart.

Over time, God's grace began to empty into my softened heart like sun and water nurturing a sapling. Eventually, the condition of my heart matured to the point that it could receive grace as I went through difficulty. I didn't have to consciously work at it; I was reflexively open to grace. Instead of trials causing me to look for ways to be good enough to prevent future trials, or causing so much shame I couldn't relate to God face to face, I started instinctively looking and waiting for God's care and involvement when I experienced affliction. Because my heart was growing toward maturity, it was soft and open to God's grace that helped me find more of it.

As my heart softened, it stimulated my redemptive imagination. Instead of seeing all the reasons I should try harder, or all the reasons God was mad at me, I began to recognize ways He was helping me and wanted to help me further. I began to anticipate His caring involvement, and I was more prepared to take help from Him or others, help I previously couldn't recognize.

In the aftermath of my brother's suicide, I realized my heart was receptive and could respond to God's grace through a time of need. In the hardest season of my life, I was open to God's grace, and it helped me stay alive through ongoing anguish.

Three

Developing a Receptive Heart

*B*ecoming receptive to God's grace isn't as easy as we often imagine. We think, "Who wouldn't take help when they need it?" However, it's often not that simple. As an extreme example, I've sat with more than one person who was clearly in the throes of an addiction that brought untold chaos into their lives. Friends stepped up for them with financial provision, child care, and other such measures so they could go to treatment—and yet they refused. I had one person tell me they didn't want to go to a recovery center because it was in a state they didn't like. The excuses only seem foolish because the best decision was so clear. Yet all of us do the same thing, whether it's refusing help for an addiction or with carrying in the groceries. We find reasons to push away kindness, and this reinforces our pride and self-reliance while keeping our heart hard and allergic to vulnerability.

Prideful Independence

We forget how easily and subtly pride pulls and prods us away from God's goodness. Pride was the energizing force behind the fall of humanity, and it's what continues to alienate us from the Lord.

Adam and Eve were first pulled into sin because Satan's suggestion inflated their ego. In tempting them to eat the fruit God told them not to,

17

Satan said, "God knows that your eyes will be opened as soon as you eat it, and you will be like God, knowing both good and evil." (Genesis 3:5)

He suggested that God would be threatened by Adam and Eve being like Him. They were pulled into rebellion through an appeal to their pride, and in Satan's presence that pride entered their thinking.

Afterward, we see pride in Adam's next response. After he'd eaten that forbidden fruit, God went looking for him. Coming upon him, the Lord called out to Adam: "Where are you?" Adam replied, "I heard You walking in the garden, so I hid. I was afraid because I was naked." (3:9–11)

Instead of humbly turning toward God when he realized he was naked, Adam turned to himself and found fig leaves to cover his nakedness. God pursued Adam and exposed the lies Adam was nurturing in his head. He invited Adam to open his heart, but Adam was having none of it. God then asked him, "Who told you that you were naked? Have you eaten from the tree whose fruit I commanded you not to eat?"

Adam replied, "It was the woman you gave me who gave me the fruit, and I ate it." (3:11–12) He followed his pride and blamed his actions on Eve.

Pride is also what got Satan booted out of God's company. Somehow after being created, Satan became lost in his own beauty. Of this the prophet Isaiah wrote, "How you are fallen from heaven, O shining star, son of the morning! . . .For you said to yourself, 'I will ascend to heaven and set my throne above God's stars . . . I will climb to the highest heavens *and be like the Most High.*'" (Isaiah 14:12–14)

Pride corrupted Satan and deceived him into thinking less of God and His ways. Like Satan, we can so easily get lost in our pride. "In all his scheming, the wicked person arrogantly thinks, 'There's no accountability, since there's no God.'" (Psalm 10:4 csb)

Pride is the inner movement away from God that makes our self-reliance seem necessary. It's a posture the evil one (Satan) wants us to adopt as a way of life. In whatever way we become our own savior by covering our nakedness instead of staying open before God, we make ourselves too important. We lose the life-giving nourishment that comes from God's grace.

By contrast, consider Jesus, who disarmed evil by humbly trusting his Father. Jesus took the "humble position of a slave" and "humbled himself in obedience to God." (Philippians 2:7–8)

In fact, the Gospels record only one occasion when Jesus provided a character quality description of Himself, and this is what He said: "I am humble and gentle at heart." (Matthew 11:29)

The battle between good and evil is often a battle between pride and humility, with pride as the key obstacle that keeps us from God's grace. "God opposes the proud but gives grace to the humble." (1 Peter 5:5)

The grace in ongoing trails or affliction is that they invite us to forsake pride by humbly opening our heart and casting our lot with God.

Three Types of Hearts

To begin understanding how to stand up to pride and grow in receptiveness to God's grace, let's envision three types of hearts.

The first is a hardened heart—one that is physically alive but spiritually dead. It's beating and content to stay that way without recognizing its spiritual condition. Such a heart is full of fleshly pride and cannot maintain the vulnerability needed to receive God's grace.

There are two motivating forces in the believer's heart: our flesh (or sinful nature), and the Holy Spirit. This is a reality that Paul articulated well to the Galatians: "So I say, let the Holy Spirit guide your lives. Then you won't be doing what your sinful nature craves. The sinful nature wants to do evil, which is just the opposite of what the Spirit wants. And the Spirit gives us desires that are the opposite of what the sinful nature desires. These two forces are constantly fighting each other, so you are not free to carry out your good intentions." (Galatians 5:16–17)

Our sinful nature reinforces prideful inclinations and makes depending on ourselves seem reasonable and necessary. It's an unseen, subtle voice inside all our hearts that wants us to live independently of God's grace. As we follow it, our heart stays closed and hard. In that posture, we don't recognize our need for God's grace and aren't limber enough to receive it. If our heart is hardened, we aren't aware of inner temptation that reinforces our pride, nor do we battle against it.

Paul spoke to this condition when he wrote, "For the sinful nature is always hostile to God. It never did obey God's laws, and it never will." (Romans 8:7)

Sadly, it's very possible to exist in a condition where we're self-satisfied and unaware of our need for God's grace. In that state, our heart is hard, and we survive by pridefully and consistently depending on ourselves and the manageable resources at our disposal.

A second type of heart is a "congested" heart, one that's physically alive but spiritually hampered. If our heart is in this condition, we begin to recognize our need for God's grace but are hampered by large amounts of pride and self-reliance. Spiritually, it's like we have coronary artery disease. We have a buildup of sinful flesh, just like a physical buildup of cholesterol and fatty deposits inside the arteries. With that kind of buildup, arteries in a physical heart become clogged or damaged, which limits or stops blood flow to the heart muscle. The heart is beating, but it isn't healthy.

When we're in this condition spiritually, the thickening of the sinful nature reinforces pride and hinders vulnerability, so the Spirit doesn't flow readily into our heart. The Holy Spirit works against our flesh and helps us recognize pride, and when we follow it we become more receptive to God's grace.

However, we need time and help to follow the Spirit and clean out a congested heart. Such a heart has opened to God, but it's easily constricted by pride. A congested heart is easily tossed back and forth between self-reliance and trust in God.

If we have a spiritually congested heart, but begin to endure well through trials, we'll awaken and become more receptive to God's grace. Over time as we're humbled, our heart is softened. A softened heart can maintain vulnerability and regularly receive God's grace. It isn't constricted by large deposits of pride. This is the third type of heart.

A softened heart is malleable, and much of its prideful flesh has been cleared out. With significantly less buildup of the sinful nature, a soft heart is humble without knowing it. It's open to God and to integrating His grace and quickly receiving it. It doesn't have to fight through pride as much, and is regularly encouraged. A receptive heart, because it receives a free flow of God's Spirit, is strong and alive.

This is what I experienced as I grieved my brother's suicide. Even though I was sad and unsettled, I kept receiving grace that gave me life and helped me demonstrate love and peace. I was humbler and more receptive to the Lord and His grace, so the Spirit flowed unhindered into my heart bringing life.

Welcoming Trials

To develop a soft heart, our relationship with trials must change. When the disciple James wrote, "When troubles of any kind come your way, consider it an opportunity for great joy" (James 1:2), he was guiding us toward a new mindset about struggles. Instead of pushing them away, we must learn to welcome them. Welcoming is not pretending they're easy, or feigning joy over the fact that they've come. Responses like that fail to grasp the mood of James' advice.

Because it's so natural to think that we shouldn't have to encounter trials, or that somebody's to blame for causing them, it takes time to grow into consciously welcoming them. We often feel shame or condemnation when we encounter difficulty because it exposes our neediness. In those moments, we'll be tempted to feed into pride. And like Adam and Eve, we'll blame someone or something else for the trouble. Welcoming trials involves the courage to accept how they expose our need for something we cannot manufacture, so that our self-reliance is revealed and weakened.

When affliction strikes us, the evil one wants us to turn inward to self and away from God, so he condemns us for any trouble we face. The aim of this condemnation is to make us we believe we're on our own to counteract and remove the affliction. This pushes us away from God's grace and saps our desire for Him to meet us in our hardship.

The Gospel of Luke records Jesus addressing a crowd about this very issue. In Luke 13:1–5, Jesus cites two examples of public tragedies—religious worshipers killed by Pilate, and eighteen people killed by a tumbling tower. Jesus asks the crowd if these people died because they were horrible sinners. Jesus's question uncovers a typical response that surrounds human tragedy. His listeners were thinking, *People suffer because of their behavior. They died because they did something wrong.*

Likewise, if we can find a direct reason to explain why we experience affliction, we have something to work on to prevent future troubles. This gives us an illusion of control and keeps us from welcoming trials. We often reduce the mystery of living in a fallen world by blaming ourselves or someone or something else when affliction comes our way. We turn away from God.

After questioning his listeners in Luke 13, Jesus concluded that they too needed to turn to God (13:5) and He lets us know that tragic events are not a sign that we did something wrong; they're a reminder to keep turning toward Him in faith.

Standing Up in Difficulty

For some reason, this truth is often obscured in Christian community. We tend to hold up those who don't have troubles in their life as being mature, while we marginalize those who struggle.

I remember the first time I began welcoming afflictions for how they could expose my pride. Early in my freshman year of college, I began engaging my faith meaningfully for the first time. During that season, I also experienced the tearing down of idols that had helped me cover pain. Throughout my elementary school, middle school, and high school years, I hid any feelings of shame or inadequacy with academic and athletic accomplishments. I'd been able to achieve much of what I set my mind to, but I had too many concussions to play football in college, I didn't make the basketball team, and I had no desire to continue running track (the other high school sport I played). Although I'd been a strong math and science student in high school, in college I had trouble keeping my head above water amid a collection of outstanding math and science students. For the first time in my life, my idols of academic and athletic achievement were out of reach.

I remember walking out of calculus class the spring of my freshman year. I'd just spent another fifty minutes listening to a professor explain something in what seemed a foreign language. I didn't understand one thing he said. If I'd encountered a moment like that in the past, I would have beat myself up for being stupid, or planned to double down and work even harder. But this time, I stepped over some pride and agreed with a nudge from the Holy Spirit, as I whispered, *"At least this keeps me dependent on You, Lord."*

Prior to that season in my life, if I'd recognized a weakness or sinful tendency, or was hurting for any reason, I would have focused on something I could do to make it better. I'd never recognized or accepted my own powerlessness. Because I could no longer hide behind performance, I was invited to stand against the pride I'd reinforced my whole life. I was beginning to recognize how determined I was to hide my insufficiency.

In addition, the pain of inadequacy helped me pay attention to things I'd missed in the past—such as how self-righteous I was. I'd believed the only thing necessary to reach my goals was hard work. In my first semester at the Merchant Marine Academy, I received lower grades than I was used to. It was humbling, considering my grades prior to that point in my life. I purposed to work much harder the next semester, so I would get higher grades. Instead, I got even lower grades, and I never had a semester as good as my first one. Covering inadequacy with academic and athletic achievement was no longer possible. I endured four years of academic and athletic mediocrity.

I remember walking out of a physics class after getting another low grade on a test. A classmate asked me what grade I got on the test; and after disclosing it, I felt his self-righteousness glare as he shared his superior grade. My life flashed before me, and I realized how many of those glances I'd given others in the past. I began to see how my version of the fig leaves of achievement had intensified through the years, hardening me and reinforcing self-reliant temptations. I'd developed a closer relationship with achievement than with God, and my heart was congested.

It was hard to recognize self-righteousness and to consider how this wounded others I'd related to in the past, but it was necessary for my heart to soften. It was a challenge to resist pride and recognize inner ugliness, but it softened my heart and prepared me for surprises ahead. As I accepted that I was a below-average math and science student, my heart was opened to nourishment much more satisfying than self-reliance.

Trials as a Tutor

My brother's suicide was twenty-nine years after I started college and began to be trained by afflictions. While I cannot say I welcomed all affliction that came my way for those twenty-nine years, I did develop an ability to resist prideful temptations and to let the ugliness in my own heart stay out in the open. I learned how to have a different relationship with trials that revealed my nakedness. As I slowly welcomed trouble as something that could eventually bring forth good, my heart softened and became more receptive, which helped me move toward depending on God's grace as a way of life.

Trials are reminders that we need help. God wants to be intimately involved with us, but we must grow the vulnerability necessary to keep our heart open to Him. He doesn't force His help on us when we trust ourselves, but He loves to be our life and support as we receive His care. Maybe guilt comes to the surface as we recognize how we've marginalized God when things were good. Maybe we feel anger that life has gotten difficult and isn't going our way, so we pull away from God. Maybe we feel heightened shame because we think we did something to deserve the difficulty and cannot imagine looking at God face to face. Let's resist the pride that turns us in on ourselves, and instead allow any guilt, anger, or shame to stay out in the open for God to meet it with His kindness.

Trials can help us get in touch with the residue that keeps us from God's grace. As we welcome them, we flush out hardened remnants in our congested heart, and we experience more of God's grace.

Four

Reviving a Hungry Heart

I love going out to dinner. In fact, I'm pretty sure food was my best friend for decades. It seemed to give me reliable comfort more than anything or anyone, and I had a hard time breaking up with it. Food was a trusty idol.

However, my enjoyment of a good dinner was complicated by the fact that I couldn't endure hunger pangs. In anticipation of enjoying dinner out in the evening, I ate light meals and snacks all day. Then during the often long wait to get seated at the restaurant, and a longer wait for dinner to arrive at our table, I filled up on appetizers and bread. By the time dinner finally arrived, I was so satiated, I was too full to enjoy the meal. Years later, as I developed enough patience to endure the anticipatory hunger pangs, I was able to wait for the main course, and I had room in my stomach to enjoy it!

Eating out at a restaurant can be a simple test of how much we dislike the feeling of vulnerability when we are forced to wait, unlike at home where we can usually go to the kitchen and find something to eat. Handling our "hunger" pangs and cravings in life maturely can be a challenge—yet God calls us to this posture: "Blessed are those who hunger and thirst for righteousness, for they will be filled." (Matthew 5:6 csb)

More than anything else, trials invite us to hunger and thirst for all that's right, because they expose so much of what we trust that isn't good or doesn't feel comfortable. To humbly endure our challenges, even while hungering and thirsting, can birth in us an ability to welcome all that is good.

After Peter reminds his persecuted readers that "God opposes the proud but gives grace to the humble," he tells them, "Humble yourselves under the mighty power of God, and *at the right time* He will lift you up in honor." (1 Peter 5:6)

Peter reminds them to wait and bear up under the suffering they faced. He recognizes how encountering trials will bring out into the open the parts of ourselves we've hidden in shame, places we need to expose to God so we can be restored. Instead of turning into ourselves, God wants us to stay open to Him.

Humbling ourselves under God's mighty hand can be understood as waiting for God's grace while our trials reveal our fears and unbelief. Such trials help us get in touch with hunger in our heart. Peter knew persecution would tempt his readers to turn back, but he urged them to stay open to the desires that the trials brought to the surface. He didn't want them to be surprised that they were hungry for more. In fact, later in his epistle, he writes, "Dear friends, don't be surprised at the fiery trials you are going through, as if something strange were happening to you." (1 Peter 4:12)

You and I aren't likely facing the same persecution that New Testament believers sometimes did, but we face trials every day that expose sinful tendencies. We too don't need to be surprised, as the poverty of our heart comes out into the open, to find we are also hungry and thirsty for more.

Staying Open

The less surprised we are as we encounter trials, the more we can actually welcome the opportunities they provide, as they help awaken and fortify our desire for God's grace. Pride turns us in on ourselves and can even atrophy our desire to be cared for by someone else. If the distressing situations we encounter cause us to shut down, become discouraged, and stop looking for assistance, we won't maintain life-giving union with God, who is the source of all our comfort.

This is part of what Jesus means when he says, "Keep on asking, and you will receive what you ask for. Keep on seeking, and you will find. Keep on knocking, and the door will be opened to you." (Matthew 7:7)

In a fallen world, it's hard to stay open to our longing for God to care about us—to keep asking, seeking, and knocking—but it softens and fortifies our heart so we're able to receive more of God's grace.

Not surprisingly, right after Jesus encourages his listeners to stay open to desiring God's grace, He reminds them how much God loves to give them good gifts: "You parents—if your children ask for a loaf of bread, do you give them a stone instead? Or if they ask for a fish, do you give them a snake? Of course not! So if you sinful people know how to give good gifts to your children, how much more will your heavenly Father give good gifts to those who ask Him." (Matthew 7:9–11)

To paraphrase Jesus's words: In a fallen world, it's hard for us to cultivate desire for God's goodness. We go through pain that can push us toward shutting down. But as we stay open to our desire for God to care about us, our heart is strengthened to receive His grace as it comes. A soft heart is a hungry heart that stays open through difficulty and has received sustenance from God over time.

Since enduring well involves waiting for God to "lift us up in honor at the right time," we must stay open to receiving His grace where it helps, while also waiting for more care to evolve over time. That hunger for more will be with us until we are in Heaven, so for now we must learn to live with it, use it to seek grace, and trust God to give us exactly what we need. Developing the capability to live that way can be maddening—like walking along a tightrope wire. Consider a musician who wants to play in the symphony and must push through mistakes and disappointments while celebrating successes along the way. It takes time and effort for the musician to become accomplished enough to receive an invitation to play in the symphony. He must push through many moments of lack before he tastes what he was longing for.

It's painful but necessary to accept that we're not supposed to have all our wants and needs met completely in this world. "If our hope in Christ is only for this life, we are more to be pitied than anyone in the world." (1 Corinthians 15:19)

Learning to live with hunger and thirst in many areas helps to train us not to bite and devour any possible good that comes our way. Letting lesser good pass by can often train us to sense and notice something better, and to enjoy it more fully when it arrives.

Feeling More Not Less

The fact that our feelings energize our longings is one reason it's so hard to get better at growing more comfortable with hungering and thirsting. It's amazing how consistently we're taught to hide or minimize our hunger because it exposes our feelings. As a counselor and teacher, I've observed how many people are uncomfortable talking about their feelings. This is usually because we are unable to control our feelings, and they bring us in touch with our deep-rooted vulnerability. So we safely package our longings (and the feelings they surface) away in a safe spot. Opening up to and admitting what we desire can feel risky, unsafe, even foolhardy. The fear of such exposure is daunting.

We ask questions like, "Can I trust my feelings?" Given that our feelings are a part of our fallen human nature, we cannot trust them with complete certainty. But consider that this is no different from every other part of ourselves. We don't ask questions like, "Can we trust our feet?" even though we trip and fall. We're more apt to "trust" our feet, because falling and experiencing physical pain seems much less scary than a broken heart. Feelings are so much harder to trust than feet, because they "mark" us, calling us to a deeper engagement with God.

Treating our feelings as untrustworthy prevents us from reaching out to God with our hungry hearts. Some type of Christian groups splinter along lines drawn by whatever human faculty the group deems most important. We know rationalists ("We just need to think better thoughts"), legalists ("We just need to choose and do the right things"), and feelers ("We just need more passion for God"). Each of these groups depends on one dimension of our personhood more than any other, instead of humbly trusting the Lord to redeem and reconcile *all* our parts.

In clarifying the importance of our whole heart over our intellect, James K. A. Smith writes in *You Are What You Love*: "Jesus is a teacher who doesn't just inform our intellect but forms our very loves. He isn't content to simply deposit new ideas into your mind; he is after nothing less than your wants, your loves, your longings. His 'teaching' doesn't just touch the calm, cool, collected space of reflection and contemplation; he is a teacher who invades the heated, passionate regions of the heart."

Our Creator designed us with the capacity to think, choose, and feel for a reason. Each faculty is a valuable part of our design, just like our ears, feet, or hands. Without feelings, we cannot cultivate loving relationships with God and others.

Forsaking Denial

If we try to be proudly independent, denying and avoiding feelings, we will in essence congest our heart and hinder the free flow of God's grace. In their book, *Cry of the Soul*, Dan Allender and Tremper Longman write, "Emotion propels us into the tragic recognition that we are not home." We avoid or deny feelings because they tend to open our eyes to the unimaginable reality of a broken world, and our need for help beyond what we can manufacture. It's a reality the evil one desperately tempts us to escape. Emotions like jealousy, rage, sorrow, and angst provide everyday reminders that *everything is not okay*, and they get us in touch with our desire for a better home. To deal with the unmanageability of harder emotions, we choose emotions that give us a sense of control to push the harder ones away.

Many of the spouses I work with in marital counseling often voice their anger or contempt instead of their fear. Anger and contempt limit our hunger by placing responsibility for our pain on someone else. On the other hand, fear is a much more vulnerable emotion. It invites us to admit our hunger. Feeling it opens our heart to possibilities we don't want to consider and reminds us we need more help than we can produce on our own.

It's easier to call our spouse "a mean jerk" than to say, "My fear is that you'll never really care about me." Turning away from self-protection toward God means vulnerably voicing what's inside us, and vulnerably getting in touch with our hunger.

Because trials and afflictions pierce our heart and bring forth feelings, they're an invitation into buried emotions and longings we want to keep hidden. I've watched this happen often with young, about-to-be mothers who experienced a miscarriage. For many of them, a miscarriage is the first large and personal loss of their life. On the other side of a miscarriage, many of them have said, "I didn't realize how much I wanted to have a baby." In addition, as they're invited to grieve the loss of a child, the softening in their hearts invites other past losses to come to the surface. They may start remembering a friend who died in high school or feel anew the distance in their relationship with their mother. As these other losses come to the surface, it helps them see how they were denying their longings and losses. As the miscarriage helps them begin grieving, they can feel emotional hunger pangs or they may stuff them back down. If they stuff them back down, their hearts harden to God's grace.

Listen again to Allender and Longman: "There are times when lack of emotion is the byproduct of hardness and arrogance. The Scriptures reveal that this absence of feelings is often a refusal to face the sorrow of life and the hunger for heaven; it is not the mark of maturity, but rather the boast of evil."

For our hardened heart to soften, we must open up to vulnerable emotions as they expose our need. The sin, suffering, and loss we experience in a fallen world are a consistent invitation to arouse feelings that can lead us to more of God's grace, if we acknowledge and entertain the hunger pangs they surface.

A Hungry Man

To illustrate what staying open and hungry looks like under trial, let's consider one man's story. John, a forty-five-year-old husband and father of two, was caught embezzling money, which caused a company to go bankrupt. He hurt people, lost his financial security, brought down a company, and will most likely face imprisonment. He cannot possibly mend all the internal or external damage he caused. Humbling himself under the mighty power of God involves opening the eyes of his heart to see and empathize with those hurt by his betrayal, and acknowledging that he cannot fix the relational and financial damage he caused. To soften to God's grace, he must recognize his hunger and thirst. As he acknowledges the way his sin hurt others, he's owning his spiritual malnourishment by opening the wounds of his heart. Recognizing and feeling the damage he caused, and giving others freedom to speak to him about this, means that he'll recognize more of his debt to others, not less. Therefore, any repair and reconciliation will require more grace from God, not less.

Consider how hard this could become for John with those he loves, who face major losses and changes. He'll naturally long for his children to respect and love him despite his failure, but it will take time for them to grow into this—if it ever happens. In the meantime, he'll have to fight through unpleasant moments while encountering their injured hearts. This is what it means to be hungry and thirsty.

Perhaps after going out to dinner with his teenage son, he's at home replaying their conversation in his mind. John hears his son say that he's expending extra effort to be honest and up front in all his dealings so that no one thinks he's like his dad. To nurture his own hunger and thirst, John accepts his son's words, which are simmering in his mind as he drifts off to sleep.

Feeling the pain in those words, and letting God hold and carry him through this trial, will help his heart soften and strengthen as grace pushes through and cleans out the deposits of pride. This helps create an atmosphere around John that invites his son to move toward him. As he lets God's grace soothe his guilt, it gives him strength to let his son experience disappointment and heartache.

Letting God's grace soften his guilt, while holding onto the hope of reconciliation with his son, keeps his heart oriented toward the Lord, and helps him persevere through difficulty. As he receives care from God along the way, and keeps desiring more at the same time, it strengthens his ability to wait for a future he himself cannot make happen.

Becoming hungry is hard work. John will be tempted to shut down his longings, because his longings got him into trouble in the first place. That's what enticed him toward embezzling the money. Such a person might think, "Wanting more than what I had got me into trouble. It would have been better if I'd just lowered my expectations."

If he shuts down his hunger for more, he'll stifle his desire for life-giving relationship with his son to be restored. That would congest his heart and push his son away.

John's longing for more didn't get him into trouble; what got him into trouble was his ongoing cooperation with lies that told him that more would come if he took matters into his own hands. Believing that his longings are the problem will only turn him toward himself and away from God and others.

Hunger Brings God's Affirmation

For John, staying hungry over time will be hard, but it will help him disarm prideful idols. We love quick fixes that make us feel full. That's one of the reasons we choose idols—they take us away from the tension of waiting. One of the reasons John embezzled money was his propensity to find quick fixes that solidified his idolatry. He regularly acted better and pretended to be more competent than he was, and refrained from situations (or covered them over) that exposed his nakedness. He couldn't let those he loved see his neediness. For instance, his wife suggested she wanted to get out of town as a family for spring break. This made John feel insecure, because they didn't have the money to do it. So he lied and said, "I have a bonus coming up that we can use to do it." He put the vacation on a credit card, and couldn't pay it off the following month. His debt increased, and the deception and resulting stress hardened his heart toward God and his family.

Going forward, instead of lying, John will have to accept limitations that invite the idol he has made of himself out into the open. At crucial times he must learn to trust God to meet the disappointments of those he loves. He can't be God to those he loves; he needs more of God to be with those he loves. His heart needs nourishment from God to disarm his insecurity. To lean into this, he will have trying periods when he goes through the types of hunger and thirst he avoided in the past and waits for God to exalt him at the proper time. To surrender to waiting like that is actually courageous behavior.

Our faith is strengthened as we endure through inadequacy and receive God's grace. So we must refute the addiction to finding what we can control to numb our pangs of hunger. Like John, staying open to God by trusting that goodness and unfailing love will pursue us all the days of our life (Psalm 23:6) will help us remember that any future good we want is God's responsibility, not ours. Resting in God's unseen and ongoing involvement—even though it means staying hungry—helps us become softer and more welcoming to those we love. That's why faith pleases God so much. It helps us navigate a fallen world.

Satan's most consistent lie is that God doesn't care about us, or that we're so bad that we're beyond God's care. Evil wants afflictions to confirm our belief in these lies. In staying open to God through afflictions and the hunger they bring, we confront the enemy by saying, "It would be easy to believe your lies when I experience affliction, but instead of allowing hunger to drive me toward you and your ways, I'll let it open me to God and His grace. When God seems most uncaring, yet I stay open to Him, His goodness pours into my needy heart and fills me with more of Himself. Hunger is a good thing."

We find this posture celebrated in the pages of Scripture, and I can't emphasize enough how strongly God affirms those who honestly hold closely onto their hunger. The writer of Hebrews speaks of them: "All these people died still believing what God had promised them. They did not receive what was promised, but they *saw it all from a distance and welcomed it.*" (Hebrews 11:13)

Welcoming God's promises is an internal, relational posture that gets strengthened through ongoing hunger. Those saints were letting a taste of heaven enter their congested hearts as they hurt and longed in a fallen world, and it increased their hope of one day being with God in fullness.

We feel discomfort only because we somehow know we were made for something better. As we ache and turn toward the Lord, we soften our heart and cleanse our spiritual arteries. The author of Hebrews goes on to say that those who welcomed God's promises—even though they hadn't received them all—were experiencing hunger like "aliens and foreigners," because "they were looking for a better place, a heavenly homeland."

Then he boldly writes, "That is why God is not ashamed to be called their God, for He has prepared a city for them." (Hebrews 11:16)

God's grace flows toward those who let this world hurt them so much that they feel out of place. He's not ashamed to be called their God. When we're living in the paradox of enduring through difficulty and staying hungry, we're shouting with our life that God cannot and will not forget us. We're humbling ourselves under His mighty power and waiting for Him to exalt us at the proper time. He—and not the evil one—will have the last word, and it will be victory over sin, suffering, and loss. And as we live in that, He affirms us.

Five

Maintaining
a Vulnerable Heart

*I*t isn't easy to maintain a posture where we learn to accept trials, nurture hunger in our heart, and wait for God to lift us up to honor. In moments of trial, our connection to God can seem to be on precarious ground. The evil one will tempt us to turn into ourselves and away from waiting on him. That's why Peter encourages vulnerable believers to "stand firm against him, and be strong in your faith." (1 Peter 5:9)

He knew that the evil one would play on the insecurity we encounter when trials come our way.

When we read an admonition to be strong in our faith, it's natural to think that means something like, "Convince yourself that God is for you," or, "Try harder to get closer to Him." That's the opposite of vulnerable trust. It's more like self-reliance and turning into ourselves. In reality, being strong in faith is an admonition to remember that God cares about us and wants to help us. Nourishing our faith as trials come our way means looking for God's support, which we cannot earn or deserve, while trusting that He wants to be with us in a way that isn't quickly discernible.

Jesus, more than anyone, knew how painful it was to feel alone and to experience a sense of rejection that comes with enduring trials. He was mobbed and nearly thrown over a cliff in His hometown (Luke 4:29). He lived with the constant knowledge of His upcoming rejection and suffering (Matthew 21:42; Luke 17:25). As He wrestled in soul-crushing grief on the night before His certain torture and death, and pleaded for support from the friends closest to Him, they could only sleep (Matthew 26:38–40). In the wrenching trials he endured, He knew he needed his Father's support to fulfill his calling.

Given the utter loneliness Jesus encountered, and how much He knew we needed relational support, He wanted his apostles to understand something very clearly before He left this world. He assured them that He would not leave them forever, but would come to them and help them with their own experience of powerlessness and aloneness: "I will ask the Father, and He will give you another Advocate, who will never leave you . . . No, I will not abandon you as orphans—I will come to you . . . I am telling you these things now while I am still with you. But when the Father sends the Advocate as my representative—that is, the Holy Spirit—He will teach you everything and will remind you of everything I have told you." (John 14:16–26)

The Holy Spirit is right here with us, and we aren't orphans. Especially in our trials, it's important to remember that the Holy Spirit will be present to us—encouraging us and helping us stay open to God's grace.

The Holy Spirit Helps in Weakness

One of the primary roles of the Holy Spirit is to come to our aid in difficulty and to help us grow into our adoption as God's children. When we're navigating through trials, the Holy Spirit is working to push back the lies of the evil one who is always attempting to take advantage of our vulnerable state and sabotage our trust in God's love.

In encouraging his readers to step toward and into the Spirit, Paul reminds them of a central function of the Holy Spirit: "You have not received a spirit that makes you fearful slaves. Instead, you received God's Spirit when He adopted you as his own children. Now we call Him, 'Abba, Father.' For *his Spirit joins with our spirit to affirm that we are God's children.*" (Romans 8:15–16)

Notice that our being affirmed by the Holy Spirit as God's children is a supernatural experience. We can't see it happening or make it happen. It happens on our behalf. The Holy Spirit works to help us remember that we aren't slaves who must beg for God's help—but we're His children, and He *wants* to help us.

"Abba Father" is an intimate term, like "Daddy." Whenever we need to, we can cry out to Him, "Daddy, Daddy!," a childlike cry of groaning. We easily forget that we're supposed to relate to God like little children. The disciples once approached Jesus and inquired about who among them was the greatest. Like good grown-ups, the disciples were aligning themselves for power and position. Jesus confronted this by replying, "I tell you the truth, unless you turn from your sins and become like little children, you will never get into the Kingdom of Heaven." (Matthew 18:3)

Instead of reaching a place where we're secure and self-reliant adults, we're supposed to work backward and become like young children looking for someone to take care of us. The hunger in our hearts for someone to care about us is good, but evil rails against it.

In this world, it's not even easy for children to be children. I experienced this early and often in my parenting. For example, one night when my oldest daughter, Aimee, was about seven years old, I was awakened around two o'clock in the morning by the sound of her stirring in her room. I went into her room to attend to her needs, and she said, "Daddy, I wasn't feeling well, and I didn't want to wake you up."

As a typical firstborn, she was trying to be overly responsible. I knew I needed to teach her how to grow comfortable with wanting and accepting help. I said to her, "I'm your dad, and I'm supposed to get up in the middle of the night and help you, even if it's a sacrifice."

Surprisingly, even as a young child she needed reinforcement to accept sacrificial help, because a lying voice inside her head was telling her she should handle it on her own.

Only a few short years before that, Aimee knew what to do when she was hurting. She cried out for parental care. She didn't spend time assessing whether she needed our help or not, or whether it would inconvenience us. She unashamedly and passionately cried for help when she needed it. The cries were painful—often piercingly painful. She felt powerless and alone and needed comfort, so she cried out for us. When she expressed powerlessness and aloneness like a child, she was treating us like parents. Yet only a couple of years later, she was already battling temptation to decide whether *she* should be the parent. She was already fighting that deceiving voice that discouraged her from reaching out for help. My job as a parent was to help her move back toward vulnerability.

Growing into maturity doesn't mean we become self-sufficient adults; it means we learn to discern between the need to push through and the need to take help.

Groaning Connects Us with the Holy Spirit

Groaning is a biblical term for the unguarded cry of an infant who anticipates their parent coming to soothe their ache—a spiritual discipline that Paul encourages every believer to practice. As we groan, the Spirit ministers God's love to us and fights condemnation for us in places we cannot.

Groaning connects our spirit with the Spirit who is the seal of our adoption. In counseling believers to unite with the Holy Spirit, Paul encourages them to groan: "For we know that all creation has been groaning as in the pains of childbirth right up to the present time. And *we believers also groan*, even though we have the Holy Spirit within us as a foretaste of future glory, for we long for our bodies to be released from sin and suffering. We, too, wait with eager hope for the day when God will give us our full rights as His adopted children." (Romans 8:22–23)

Paul explains how the Holy Spirit helps us see things from God's perspective, which clearly reveals that we were made for a better world—making this world more painful to endure. Instead of turning in on ourselves by minimizing the pain of a fallen world, the Holy Spirit wants to safeguard us from pretending. He helps us turn toward God, reaching out for His comfort. It takes a while to learn to groan well, because we're so used to denying pain and not talking vulnerably with the Lord about how much we hurt.

In fact, when we're hurting, the Holy Spirit is crying out to God on our behalf. Because afflictions specifically expose our weakness and arouse our unbelief, the Holy Spirit comes to our aid to help us express ourselves more openly to God so we can receive His help and affirmation: "The

Holy Spirit helps us in our weakness. For example, we don't know what God wants us to pray for. But the Holy Spirit prays for us with groanings that cannot be expressed in words. And the Father who knows all hearts knows what the Spirit is saying, for the Spirit pleads for us believers in harmony with God's own will." (Romans 8:26–27)

Groaning is cooperating with the Spirit toward that end. I can think of times when I was really hurting, and I was trying to figure out the right thing to say to arouse God's attention or to get Him to care. I was acting like an orphan missing a parent, not like a child who *had* a parent. All the while, the Holy Spirit was praying through me. Instead of figuring out what and how to pray, I simply could have cried out more vulnerably for God's help and trusted the Spirit to pray with and for me.

The Holy Spirit does for us what we cannot do ourselves. He communicates with God in a way we cannot understand, but that communication helps to bring about God's will for us.

An Example of Groaning

Becoming someone who groans well is not a quick or seamless process for most people.

Consider Susan, who was betrayed by her husband. She came to me in great affliction because he'd had an affair and was leaving her. Her world, and that of her five children, was turned upside-down. In our first meeting, I could tell Susan was very turned in on herself. She rarely made eye contact, was regularly apologizing for complaining, and couldn't even say she was disappointed with her husband. She wasn't in touch with her own dignity, and she had a hard time relating in an open way. I could see she was resolute on restoring her marriage because she thought it was her only chance of really being cared for in this life. The focus of her questions centered around what she could do to get her husband back. She'd spent the bulk of the marriage denying her needs and working to come through for her husband. As she talked with me, I was sad to see her consistently forsaking the pain in her heart and subtly taking responsibility for what happened.

In that first meeting, I listened to Susan and tried to help her begin groaning by naming as much pain as she could. She awkwardly talked about a couple difficult things such as feeling ashamed around her friends and her financial fear about the future, but she rushed through them without showing much emotion or vulnerability.

We didn't get very far.

Toward the end of that session, I tried to help her begin to understand the connection between vulnerability and experiencing care from God and others, and how with the difficulty ahead she would need to lean on God and others a little bit more. I then encouraged her to spend a couple of evenings reflecting on moments when she felt something deeply, and to journal about those experiences. I knew the Holy Spirit would be helping Susan in her weakness, guiding her into the truth of how impoverished her heart was and of how much she needed God's grace. She needed help opening her heart to receive from God and others, and the Holy Spirit was there to help and guide her toward more.

Several meetings later she mentioned something about how dejected her older son had been behaving. I knew Susan would be more likely to talk about the pain her children were feeling than her own pain. That would make her feel less vulnerable. So I asked a follow-up question.

As we talked about the impact her husband's affair had on her oldest son, she began to soften. Just naming some of the pain she was carrying out loud to another human being relieved some of the weight of her life.

After a good discussion on this topic, I felt Susan resting more. I asked her how she felt when she saw her son hurting. She paused, not having much experience at voicing vulnerable emotions. I followed up my question with a statement: "When children are hurting, I find that the mother tends to hurt more than the child does."

This statement shot through Susan, and her eyes moistened. She felt seen and known.

I asked her to put words to her emotions, and she said, "I didn't even know I was sad, I was so focused on my son."

I began to dialogue with her about her pain, and she was able to express a little more. At the end of the session, I reflected on our time together and explained more openly—and with more nuance—how she could learn to groan more restfully and let God and others care for her.

Slowly, the truth about what she'd suffered began to surface, and Susan opened her heart more fully. That brought changes in day-to-day living. For instance, she reported making time to take a walk with a friend who'd been reaching out to her more regularly. She recounted sharing shameful feelings with that friend and walking away feeling more hopeful and not knowing why.

I suggested that groaning with God more regularly had strengthened her heart to the point that she could reach out and experience His care through another human being.

Another time she found herself weeping to the words of a song as she drove across town. That song cut through defenses that used to be impenetrable, but were softened through months of groaning. I helped her see how God's grace had always been there, but now she was able to respond to it differently. She could see how these moments were unfolding because she was being led by and responding to the Holy Spirit's direction. Vulnerably naming the betrayal and loss in her marriage—and starting to groan—opened Susan's heart. As the Holy Spirit kept helping her in her weakness and guiding her into truth, God's grace moved from her head to her heart.

Months later, when Susan came in for another appointment. I was struck by the difference in her countenance. It was softer and more alive. She talked about pain she felt in the relationship with her husband, and she was also able to explain the void left by his departure. She was more comfortable describing her internal world with vulnerability. Her relational world had crumbled. Married friends were awkward around her, and she had no single or divorced friends. There were more nights than she could count where she drifted off to sleep feeling abandoned and resentful. She reported praying things like, "God, I hurt so much, I feel like I won't make it," or, "I can't bear the pain of hearing my children cry at the absence of their dad."

She said that those prayers felt awkward for a while and brought feelings of shame, so it didn't seem to her like she was groaning to God. Over time, Susan became more connected to what she was saying and began to experience God's presence with her in those prayers.

Talking that way to God was so foreign to her at first, it didn't seem like praying. She didn't recognize that she was praying in a much richer way than before her life crumbled. The Holy Spirit was guiding her toward a deeper sense of being God's child and experiencing His care in an effectual way. She used to pray neatly and quietly in the corner of her bedroom. But after months of practicing at groaning, there would be several moments each day when she painfully sighed words or thoughts of torment to God—which I suggested were much richer prayers than the ones she used to voice nicely from the corner of her bedroom. Susan was praying more like Jesus: "While Jesus was here on earth, He offered prayers and pleadings, with a loud cry and tears, to the One who could rescue Him from death. And God heard His prayers because of His deep reverence for God." (Hebrews 5:7)

From the mood of our conversation and the look on Susan's face, it was obvious that the Holy Spirit was helping her surrender to kindness around her that she couldn't earn or deserve.

The Gospel is counterintuitive. At the very point we want to be strongest—after we've sinned the worst, or a crushing tragedy has come our way—we must become a child again and groan, letting the Spirit soften our heart so we become more receptive to God's unearned work on our behalf.

Groaning into Our Adoption

The pleading and prayers of the Holy Spirit put us in touch with God's grace that transcends our circumstances. Our fears and anxieties are often safely protected behind fig leaves of manageability or performance. Sin, suffering, and loss bring them to the surface. When we sin, we face the powerlessness of not being able to change ourselves. When we suffer, we face our inability to manipulate our world. When we experience loss, we encounter a future we cannot control. As we groan through this powerlessness, and the Holy Spirit directs us and communicates with God, we become more open and responsive to His grace.

We have endless need to be reminded of God's love, which is one reason that "the Spirit searches everything, even the depths of God." (1 Corinthians 2:10 csb)

Those depths assuredly include God's love and power toward us who believe. As we groan, the Spirit is searching the depths of God's love, looking for an aspect of it that will help us more meaningfully experience our adoption into God's family.

The Holy Spirit looks for opportunities to help us recognize and respond to God's grace. Although our sinful nature inside us—and the worldly influences outside—bully us toward self-reliance and loneliness, this is undone by our groaning into God's love.

"I pray that from his glorious, unlimited resources he will empower you with inner strength *through His Spirit*. Then Christ will make His home in your hearts as you trust in Him. Your roots will grow down into God's love and keep you strong. And may you have the power to understand, as all God's people should, how wide, how long, how high, and how deep His love is." (Ephesians 3:16–18)

Because Susan went from self-reliantly trying to carry the world on her back to learning to voice when she was hurting, her heart was softening into God's grace. Groaning gets us out of ourselves and acknowledges that God is holding onto us and will not let us go.

We don't have the capacity, wisdom, or strength to convince ourselves that God loves us. That's the work of the Holy Spirit. Our job is to relate vulnerably to the Lord, and to invite the Spirit to do His job. Because "we have not received the spirit of the world, but the Spirit who comes from God, so that we may understand what has been freely given to us by God." (2 Corinthians 2:12 csb)

After Paul addresses the ministry of the Spirit and our adoption and groaning in Romans 8, he describes how inseparable we are from God's love: "Neither death nor life, neither angels nor demons, neither our fears for today, nor our worries about tomorrow—not even the powers of hell can separate us from God's love." (8:38)

Paul is eloquently describing how much the Spirit intercedes for us to take ownership of the fact that we're God's children. Paul even points his words at condemnation from the evil one that separates us from God's love: "Who then will condemn us? No one—for Christ Jesus died for us and was raised to life for us, and He is sitting in the place of honor at God's right hand, pleading for us." (8:34)

Groaning with God's Holy Spirit is how we connect to and advance that reality. When we go through our worst moments of wounding, sin, and unbelief, our heart will be pried open. In our recognized need, the

Holy Spirit can guide us into more of God's grace. This will increase our confidence that we're His child, even though we feel hopeless and alone. "For we know how dearly God loves us, because He has given us the Holy Spirit to fill our hearts with His love." (Romans 5:5)

Six

Grounding a Confused Heart

$\mathcal{F}$or many of us, groaning into a childlike posture with God is difficult because of the reservoir of conflicting and divided feelings residing in our heart. In fact, in the New Testament, James explains that the reason we get into quarrels and fights is that these evil and conflicting desires are at war within us—and even when we ask for help, we don't receive it, because our motives are all wrong, and we want only what will give us pleasure (James 4:1–3).

Our hearts are often a mixture of confusing feelings, and trials bring confusion to the surface. It's not unusual for trials to unearth emotions like resentment, anger, shame, or jealousy. Such moments are precarious because we like to pretend we don't feel such things. Instead of intensifying our denial, burying the feelings with more determination, or acting them out on others, we need God's help to steady our confused heart.

Peter anticipated the difficult emotions believers would experience as they endured affliction. He knew that yielding to persecution would be challenging for us, and that God was willing to meet us in our confusion. Therefore, right after he counsels his readers to humble themselves under God's mighty power, he tells them to "cast all their anxieties on Him, because He cares for them." (1 Peter 5:7 esv)

The Greek verb for "cast" here is the same as the one for "threw" in Luke 19:35—"They brought the colt to Jesus and threw their garments over it for Him to ride on." When we're suffering, Peter invites us to throw our concerns upon God in a similar manner, because God is strong and loving enough to handle it.

Why would God encourage us to do that with Him? We forget that God is not insecure, afraid, weak, or selfish. He's full of grace and has no problem embracing the intensity of our dark emotions. In fact, God is most gracious when He meets us in those moments. When we come to Him because we've run into trouble, God's response is what C. S. Lewis in *The Problem of Pain* calls "divine humility": "It is a poor thing to strike our colors to God when the ship is going down under us; a poor thing to come to Him as a last resort, to offer up 'our own' when it is no longer worth keeping. If God were proud He would hardly have us on such terms: but He is not proud, He stoops to conquer, He will have us even though we have shown that we prefer everything else to Him and come to Him because there is 'nothing better' now to be had."

The Courage to Be Honest

God's divine humility is awkward for us. We're not used to relating to someone so humble and kind. We reflexively believe we must relate to others properly for them to relate back to us with kindness. We assume that if we relate with too much rawness or bluntness to someone, they won't love us through it. And yet, when it comes to loving His children through affliction, God doesn't follow this pattern.

Peter acknowledges that trials expose our pride, arouse intense feelings, and bring confusion to our relationship with God. He doesn't want us thinking we must behave properly to earn God's help. If we're willing to welcome the difficulty in front of us, God will meet us with His grace and help us with the pain and bewilderment that trials bring to the surface.

As you read through the Scriptures, notice that those closest to God were honest with Him. Earlier I noted how God's own Son said, "My God, my God, why have you abandoned me?" (Matthew 27:46)

Jesus related honestly with his Father; he didn't pretend when he was in pain. Abraham, an abiding example of faith that we're to emulate, laughed at God's promise after having to wait so long to experience its fulfillment. At the ripe old age of ninety-nine, God reaffirmed His promise and its coming fulfillment to Abraham, and here's how Abraham responded: "Then Abraham bowed down to the ground, but he laughed to himself in disbelief. 'How could I become a father at the age of 100?' he thought." (Genesis 17:17)

David is very candid with God throughout the Psalms, as when he says to God, "I am ignored as if I were dead, as if I were a broken pot." (Psalm 31:12)

There are other biblical examples, but suffice it to say, those who were close to God were not afraid to be honest with Him.

God loves our honesty because it disarms relational indifference. If we turn into ourselves because we think God cannot handle our intense and confusing emotions, we become indifferent to Him. If we don't communicate with someone, that person doesn't exist for us. Yet when we bring all of who we are to God, we're making several steps of faith. We're acknowledging that it's foolish to hide anything from Him, and we're demonstrating our trust that He'll help us in our existing condition. Hiding our confusion from God will only harden our heart and hinder its receptivity. On the other hand, as we begin to express hard emotions to God and get angry or disappointed with Him—yet knowing that He still loves us—our heart is cleaned out and softened as we experience new depths of His grace. What we believed in our head moves into our heart.

Unfortunately, we can be too comfortable acting out our anger sideways at God, and we need to develop the courage to bring our confusion to Him face to face. For instance, consider Sheila, a mother who diligently serves her daughter Louise and does everything "right" to make sure Louise is happy. However, Sheila isn't aware how easily she can be controlling and demanding. It gets heated during Louise's teen years, and Louise says something disrespectful. Sheila is shocked and unloads a tirade of anger in response. She demeans Louise and shames her for questioning her "perfect" mothering. Sheila isn't aware of how much their growing separation scares her, and doesn't confront her misconception that her "perfect" parenting would prevent any disconnection between them. Instead of wrestling out her fears with God directly as she encountered them, she hid them under the pressure she kept putting on herself to be the perfect mom.

The unspoken message to the Lord through Sheila's meticulous parenting was this: "I don't trust You to protect my close relationship with my daughter, so I'll put in extra effort to maintain it."

Sheila would have been better off expressing those words directly to the Lord along the way, instead of channeling them into determination to be a perfect mom. The many moments when Sheila was afraid or angry about her tensions with Louise, she could have poured out her feelings on the Lord. Had she done that, it's more likely her anger would not have been stockpiled in such a way that it came out at her daughter after sixteen years of parenting. If Sheila had demonstrated the courage to be more honest with God along the way, it would have been a sign of respect and acknowledgment of His transcendence.

In his book, *May I Hate God?*, Pierre Wolff says, "When I freely show anger to my friend, I also show paradoxically that I believe his love is able to take it. If I cannot be myself with my friend, exactly as I am right now, for better or for worse—then with whom can I be myself? Beneath my anger my behavior says this: At least with you I can reveal myself as I am."

Lament Brings to the Surface What We've Kept Hidden

Bringing our darker emotions and thoughts to God directly is called lamenting, and it's a skill many of us have never developed, though it's clearly affirmed in the Scriptures. Trials bring out what's ugly inside us. God already knows the dark ugliness in our heart that we're blind to, and He wants us to see what's in there. He has already provided forgiveness for the worst about us—past, present, and future—but we aren't convinced of that.

In her book, *Soul Feast*, Marjorie Thompson says, "It takes practice to learn not to censor our prayer. But trying to keep secrets from God is like the three-year-old who covers her eyes and declares, 'You can't see me.' God sees into our heart more clearly than we do. Indeed, God is the one who prompts us to look at what we have swept under the rug of our repressions and rationalizations."

Job is the best example of this in the Scriptures. He was a righteous man with deep integrity (Job 1:1), but Satan accused him of behaving this way because the Lord had blessed him beyond measure (1:9–11). So the Lord permitted Satan to do what he wanted with all of Job's blessings, although He didn't allow Satan to hurt Job.

As a result, Job lost all his oxen, donkey, and farmhands, all his sheep and shepherds, all his camels and servants, and all his sons and daughters. After the enormity of that tragedy, Job responded, "I came naked from my mother's womb, and I'll be naked when I leave. The Lord gave me what I had, and the Lord has taken it away. Praise the name of the Lord!" (Job 1:21)

Those verses are held up as the "standard" that Job maintained in his relationship with God. However, that was just the beginning of the story.

After destroying all that was dear to Job, Satan said that if God let him inflict physical pain on Job, then Job would curse God. After receiving permission, Satan struck Job with boils from head to foot.

Around that time Job's, friends showed up: "When three of Job's friends heard of the tragedy he had suffered, they got together and traveled from their homes to comfort and console him . . . . When they saw Job from a distance, they scarcely recognized him. Wailing loudly, they tore their robes and threw dust into the air over their heads to show their grief. Then they sat on the ground with him for seven days and nights. No one said a word to Job, for they saw that his suffering was too great for words." (2:11–13)

For the first seven days, they were good friends as they sat with Job and took in his pain. This helped Job trust them, and after a week he poured out all his confusion with God to his friends. He complained and said things like this: "Let the day of my birth be erased, and the night I was conceived. Let that day be turned to darkness. Let it be lost even to God on high, and let no light shine on it." (3:3–4)

After Job poured out his discontent with God to his friends, they went from being good friends to bad friends. For the next twenty-eight chapters, Job and his friends grapple with each other. In essence, Job tells his friends, "I have a vertical problem. I don't understand who God is anymore. I'm confused and angry. Until He reminds me who He is, I'll have no rest."

Job wanted help wrestling with God. He wanted to lament, but his friends couldn't stand it. They tried to correct him—Eliphaz tries three times, Bildad three times, and Zophar twice. Each time, Job answers them back. At several points Job even lifts his voice to God as he converses with his friends. Job was lamenting—he acknowledged God's omniscience by bringing his pain to Him.

Finally God showed up and spoke to Job: "Who is this that questions my wisdom with such ignorant words? Brace yourself like a man, because I have some questions for you, and you must answer them." (38:2–3)

Then God gave Job a lesson on his transcendence. When he was done, Job said, "I had only heard about You before, but now I have seen You with my own eyes. I take back everything I said, and I sit in dust and ashes to show my repentance." (Job 42:5–6)

Job's heart was grounded and steadied through his encounter with God. Something good happened inside him through the process of lamenting. He went from hearing in his head to seeing in his heart. Job kept bringing all he had to God, and he poured out what was in his heart. When God finally spoke, it was painfully clear what was true. God was God, and Job was not. Job experienced more profound humility and transformation than if he hadn't lamented.

When we experience something painful, the shock and emotions don't dissipate quickly. We need someone to help us with the depth and breadth of pain that brings inner confusion. As we lament those emotions, our heart over time is growing in attachment and receptivity to those who're listening to us. When the listeners who've been taking in our pain speak to us, we have affection and respect for them, which helps us hear what they have to say. That's one of the reasons God's words transformed Job.

In addition, God didn't shame or condemn Job. Instead, He answered Job's prayers. Job had been saying, "God, you don't seem like God to me anymore. You seem weak and ineffectual. I'm angry, lost, and confused." By expressing that honestly, Job was casting his cares on God, and God responded to his integrity by showing up and kindly responding to Job's laments. He spoke kindness into Job's confusion by reminding Job that He was still God. This was an affirmation of Job's prayers, an affirmation that becomes clear in the way God rebukes Job's friends: "After the Lord had finished speaking to Job, He said to Eliphaz the Temanite: 'I am angry with you and your two friends, for you have not spoken accurately about Me, as my servant Job has.'" (Job 42:7)

Job is held up as the hero, as God exposes those friends: *You have not spoken accurately about me, as my servant Job has.* I challenge you to read for yourself what Job said to God, and see if you've ever had the courage to be that honest with God. Job knew something about God before he lamented—but through lamenting, he tasted something about God that changed him.

Lament Fosters Relational Intimacy

Lament is an important spiritual practice because it's a relational process. It opens our heart to experience the strength of God's grace. Enduring through unexplainable tragedy is not a rational or academic problem, but a relational problem. When we're hurting, it's easy to experience disorientation with the Lord, and the evil one is quick to lie to us about God's strength and love.

That is the grace in lament. God wants to help us tear down the very ways in which we've trusted ourselves and built defensive fortresses around our heart toward Him. In times of trial, the evil one intensifies such sinful heart postures, and as we bring them to God, we mock the work of the evil one.

It's impossible for us to become more like Christ in our own strength, so unguarded moments that come on the other side of affliction surface an honesty that can be transformative. We need a place to go with all the craziness we've kept hidden inside us. Trials nudge us in that direction.

Growing up, I internalized a lot of the pain in my parents' marriage. I told myself that my future wife and I would have a better marriage. For whatever reason, this became an orienting passion in my life. I wanted a marriage and family without any pain. Most of my "good behavior" prior to marriage was an effort to secure that pain-free future, but it fostered an undetected self-righteousness inside me. A good portion of it said to God, "You never should have put me in that kind of pain as a child. Now I'll do better—I'll show You and everyone else what a family looks like without pain."

51

It was foolish to think I could accomplish that in my own strength, or that I could avoid future pain on an ongoing basis. When my wife and I started struggling, my self-righteousness surfaced. Prior to marriage, I'd been trying in my angry and determined behavior to exercise control over life because I didn't trust God. As a result, I thought I'd earned a pain-free marriage with my good behavior. When we inevitably ran into problems, the pain I'd pushed down through controlled behavior came storming out of me. I raged: "God, how could You do this to me? I worked so hard to avoid this! You betrayed and fooled me. I'm furious at You!"

A crazy thing happened as I lamented to the Lord. He loved me through it. All the confusion, pain, and anger that I'd ignored and stored up inside me for more than two decades was poured out on God. That's where I moved through resentment and experienced God's care. I experienced what Jesus said about the sinful woman: "I tell you, her sins—and they are many—have been forgiven, so she has shown Me much love. But a person who is forgiven little shows only little love." (Luke 7:47)

I had no idea how much I'd been forgiven until I lamented. For years I'd been reciting how much God loved me, but I hid all my questions and resentments from Him. I never tested the depth and breadth of His love. I needed the courage to lament for His love to move from my head to my heart. Relating to God in a way that seemed disrespectful is one of the most powerful ways I experienced His grace.

Having the integrity to bring exactly what we feel to God—and trusting Him to handle it—opens up the door for His grace to move from our head to our heart.

With God, it's just as C. S. Lewis expressed it: He stoops to conquer.

Seven

Protecting a Bullied Heart

*H*ave you ever awakened from a midafternoon nap, and not known where you were? That's just like what happens to us in a fallen world. We drift off to sleep in the darkness that surrounds us, and we forget our place as God's children. We let evil lure us to sleep—a half-conscious state in which we aren't as aware of (or attuned to) what God is doing in and around us.

Paul addresses this issue when he urges the church at Ephesus to live as people of the light: "Awake, O sleeper, rise up from the dead, and Christ will give you light." (Ephesians 5:14)

It's so easy to forget that behind the scenes a cosmic war is raging all around us. This reality intensifies when we encounter trials, because they complicate our relationship with God, making them prime opportunities for us to get lost in darkness.

That's exactly why Peter tells a church going through affliction, "Stay alert! Watch out for your great enemy, the devil. He prowls around like a roaring lion, looking for someone to devour. Stand firm against him." (1 Peter 5:8–9)

Peter reminds his persecuted readers that Satan takes advantage of human suffering by pouncing on us when we're weakened. In such moments, we want to be aware of Satan's tactics, and we want to protect our hearts so they stay vulnerable and responsive to God's grace. I might restate Peter's words this way: Remember that our enemy is the ruler of this world, and he's the opposite of God. He kicks us when we're down.

When trials knock us back on our heels, Satan comes in to bully us with persecution and lies. He wants us to become more self-reliant, not less. Don't forget this, because he won't change his strategy.

Becoming more aware of how Satan preys on our vulnerability in trial helps us to safeguard our hearts so they continue to respond to God's grace and soften through difficulty. Although Peter is addressing attacks from Satan, to understand and resist him, we have to understand the broader nature of spiritual warfare—as articulated well by David Powlison in *Power Encounters*: "The epistles concentrate their attention on what we properly call spiritual warfare: our vulnerability to be taken captive to Satan to believe his lies and do his will. They present moral evil as a three-stranded braid of the world, the flesh, and the devil. Our social situation feeds us a stream of beguilements and threats; our own hearts gravitate to lies and lust; the devil schemes to aggravate sin and unbelief."

Spiritual warfare involves confronting all three components of evil—the world, the flesh, and the devil. The wounding of trials makes lies and lusts seem enticing, and if we nurture and agree with them, our heart will harden toward God. In the pain of affliction, our heart gravitates toward those lies and lusts, and the evil one will play on this by trying to torment us into sin and unbelief. However, if we're more aware of evil's schemes while under trial, we won't be as susceptible to being bullied away from God's grace.

Bullied into Prideful Patterns

Heeding Peter's advice involves remembering that Satan's fiery arrows (Ephesians 6:16) will be directed toward our prideful patterns. These patterns are ways of living based on self-reliance. They're energized by pride that congests our heart. They provide an illusion that we have control over life and don't need God. We build these prideful patterns on God-given gifts or strengths. For instance, when facing social tension an introverted child might hide behind being shy, while an extroverted one might readily morph into the life of the party. These seem like innocent ways to fit in and protect oneself. But if repeatedly chosen over time, they congest our heart by becoming fig leaves that hide the shame and fear we carry.

We can depend too much on certain personality traits or gifts to manage the awkwardness of growing up. Unfortunately, it's normal to selfishly depend on strengths God designed into our makeup. In the susceptibility of youth, we gravitate toward whatever gives us an enhanced sense of self. Because these patterns form while we're vulnerable, we fail to grasp how evil contributes to their development. Few intellectually gifted children will think, *My excellent grades don't make me better than others. My artistic classmate has a gift I don't have. The jealousy I feel when my classmate's artwork is celebrated exposes my lack and helps me see how I need to depend on God just like everyone else.*

For you, perhaps it wasn't being intellectual or artistic but some other strength that you learned to depend upon. Each of us will find whatever provides consolation. And this makes it easier for the evil one to energize our anger at how vulnerable we are growing up, and to prod us toward independence from God. "For the sinful nature is always hostile to God. It never did obey God's laws, and it never will." (Romans 8:7)

Our sinful flesh is motivated by hatred toward God. In vulnerable moments, when God seems distant or uncaring, it's easy to follow nudges that give us a sense of control without realizing they're motivated by anger.

The insecurity and threats involved in growing up and forming our identity makes trusting reliable patterns very alluring. However, managing life through our strengths dissociates us from the daily need to trust God's grace. Using our strengths to hide from rejection is so easy to choose that we may not even know we're using them to deal with our fears. The straight-A student who plunges into her studies will feel like she's being herself, and may not readily recognize self-protective behavior.

Because depending on prideful patterns feels so natural, we don't recognize the anger energizing our choices, the resentment it builds, or how this contributes to our heart being less responsive to God's grace. The more we become committed to these patterns in moments of vulnerability, the more we constrict our heart, and the less we need to depend on God's grace.

Paul is addressing this type of development when he writes, "You were dead in your trespasses and sins in which you previously walked according to the ways of this world, according to the ruler of the power of the air, the spirit now working in the disobedient." (Ephesians 2:1–2 csb)

Our trespasses and sins are actions we choose in order to reinforce prideful patterns, and they're influenced by the "ways of the world" and "the ruler of the power of the air."

The regular pressure from the world to fit in makes it easy for Satan to enflame the fleshly lust of social affirmation for the extroverted teenager. The world and the flesh are continually working together, but we see this most clearly in how the extroverted person succumbs to temptation to be funny at inappropriate times, creating social disconnection. Leaning on what sets them apart can become a reliable pattern so much that the extroverted teenager has a hard time forsaking it at an unsuitable time.

In *Power Encounters*, David Powlison addresses this: "Ephesians chiefly stresses the attacks of deception that darken and harden people. Satan establishes his moral lordship mainly through lies. The issue in view is human and moral evil. The devil's schemes seek to draw us into sin and lies, to harden and darken us, to induce us to live in the flesh."

The insecure teenager depending on prideful patterns or "living in the flesh" cannot abandon their strategy for life when someone needs caring attention.

An Example of Bullying

Understanding this background sheds light on what's going on through trials. They awaken us from our dependence on prideful patterns. As life unfolds, we fall asleep and forget we have an enemy. We dissociate from God by reflexively trusting familiar patterns, and trials knock us out of that stupor.

For trials to be redemptive in helping us become more responsive to God's grace, we need to be alert and sober to the warfare they usher in. Consider the affliction of the bereaved. If you have experienced the loss of a loved one, you know the pain can be excruciating. One day you're caught up in a relationship with someone you love—together you give and receive, laugh and cry, hope and despair—and the next day your loved one is gone. No goodbyes, no closure, no ongoing participation in life. Someone you love is ripped out of your life with no warning. You don't want to go to bed that first night, because it was the last day this loved one was in your life. You don't want to wake up the next morning, because it's the first day of your life without this person you love. The emptiness and void that comes on the other side of loss is awful.

In a fallen world, the bereaved will face the temptation to rely on their prideful patterns with more determination. When we lose someone we love, our powerlessness is exposed in full view. Consider Samantha, whose daughter Evie died in a car accident. Samantha was an overly conscientious mother, and after the accident, she was regularly swamped with condemning thoughts that if she'd bought Evie that vehicle with the higher safety rating, her daughter would still be alive. Samantha's prideful pattern is flavored with extreme amounts of conscientiousness. Throughout life, she almost always made safe and more conservative choices that reinforced an illusion of control. That's where Satan tempts and tries her, and Samantha is regularly reminded of the moment Evie looked at her for approval to purchase the more expensive car, and Samantha shook her head no. Samantha's commitment to responsible living was in conflict. Should she spend less money or get a safer car for her daughter? Both were conscientious choices. She made the choice to save money.

In the aftermath of the accident, Samantha is regularly bombarded with the thought, *You fool! You knew the more expensive car was safer.* That temptation, and others like it, consistently flood Samantha's consciousness, reminding her of everyday mishaps she made with Evie.

The evil one wants to reinforce Samantha's ongoing guilt in her grief, so she becomes more committed to being conscientious and hardens her heart. In the pain of loss, these lies are an attempt to intensify her trust in her prideful pattern, so she puts her focus there instead of surrendering into more of God's grace. Because she feels like she failed her daughter, she doesn't share the intrusive thoughts with anyone and begins to be submerged under a sea of dread, feeling responsible for her daughter's death.

The lies swirling around in Samantha's head turn her inward to self and away from God and others. God's grace is something she believes in her head but cannot access, because she's easy prey for deception in her heart. Any parent is faced with countless decisions that aren't perfectly clear as they guide their child toward adulthood. Because Samantha regularly pressured herself to take the responsible route, she can easily envision many ways she could have been more conscientious.

As Samantha stays focused on her failed choices, her heart closes and hardens to God's grace. She's grieving and vulnerable. Like many who are grieving, she often doesn't sleep well, and also feels isolated. In that condition, ongoing bullying from the evil one makes it hard for Samantha to get her head above water. In moments of buffeting by the evil one, she forgets the many other times when she was *not* perfectly conscientious and yet things turned out fine. She fails to remember times when God's grace helped her in the past, so it's harder to see it in the present. Historically she was more focused on being conscientious than being vulnerable and trusting, so when Satan condemns her for not being conscientious enough, she takes it in, hook, line, and sinker. Because she fed this prideful pattern for decades, it's hard to stay sober and remember that Satan is playing on her weakened state. His lies reinforce her illusion of control and keep her heart congested. The flow of God's grace is blocked.

The loss of her daughter could serve as an invitation for Samantha to let go of her short-sighted wall of overly conscientious behavior. In the wake of Evie's death, Samantha felt the agonizing loss both of Evie and of her assumptions of false protection. The loss invited Samantha to deeper humility and trust, but the evil one kept sending fiery darts to thwart movement in that direction.

As our prideful pattern is exposed as untrustworthy, thus making God's grace more appealing, the evil one will tempt us back toward that pride. To move ahead, Samantha must keep saying, "I was foolish to think I could have ultimately protected my daughter. I could never have been conscientious enough to provide ultimate safety in a fallen world. Lord have mercy." That type of sobriety would loosen up Samantha's prideful pattern, soften her heart, and help her be more responsive to God's grace.

Resisting the Bully

In the vulnerability of grief in a fallen world, Samantha was flooded with lies that fed her lust for control. If I was counseling Samantha, I would attempt to help her move past the evil one's schemes and grow into a sobriety that would expand the softness of her heart. For instance, Samantha might stumble into remembering a past moment of real joy she experienced with Evie, and start telling me about it. If that happened, I would ask her for a couple more examples of beautiful moments with Evie, and I would watch her soften as she felt more connected to her daughter. I might then say something like, "As we talk about Evie and remember how much she filled your life with love, I understand more clearly why the loss is so painful." At that point we could grieve together, and Samantha would experience a mixture of loss and connection. Grieving with me would help Samantha walk past evil's lies and temptations and help open her heart to receive more of God's grace to soothe some of her pain.

That's the opposite of focusing on what she could have done to prevent the loss. Reminiscing about how much she loved Evie would soften her heart and help her step out of her prideful pattern. For Samantha, it would be movement away from control and toward love and hope. Grieving with another would help her experience refreshing grace-filled tears, as she's reconnected to her love for Evie. However, as that happens, there's a good chance Satan would tempt her back toward conscientiousness. Remaining sober and resisting evil would prove difficult for Samantha.

Often as I walk others toward more vulnerable relating, they're pulled away from it. While grieving with me, Samantha could quickly shift from redemptive softening to a strained face as she agreed with a fleeting temptation: "I knew I should have gotten her a safer car!" The evil one would be quick to shoot a dart in Samantha's direction to sabotage her experience of God's grace as it soothed an aching heart.

To awaken Samantha to Satan's lies, I might say something like, "That's true; you could have done more and even gotten her a safer car. But no matter how much you did to be conscientious, there still would have been something you missed. However, it's not true that you're responsible for her death. I know you well enough to know you cared for her and brought her life, not death. It was good to remember Evie and grieve together over how much you lost. I want you to stay with feelings of loss and love."

Samantha loved Evie, so her absence was painful. There was no way to minimize that. Covering over pain with a false sense of control embedded in her conscientious prideful pattern would keep her from God's grace and comfort. I would step in to help her become more alert to the strategy of evil. In trials, Satan plays on our vulnerability by lying to us and appealing to our fleshly lust for control. He plays on our prideful patterns. Agreeing with lies from Satan that she should have and could have done more to keep Evie alive kept Samantha lost in her flesh and congested in heart. She needed help recognizing and becoming conscious of Satan's ploy.

Satan cannot create or give life; he can only deceive and bully. He corrupts God's good creation. God provides each of us with gifts and strengths to help us connect with others and have impact in this world.

Samantha was a good woman, and she loved Evie well. Her conscientiousness provided a lot of safety and rest for her daughter in good ways. Samantha didn't realize—until her conscientiousness was not enough to protect Evie from death—that she'd attached too much to the affirmation and distinction it brought her. It gave her a false sense of control and mastery over her world, and this made it harder for Samantha to be receptive to God's grace. Turning away from that would be one way to honor the life of her daughter. If she did that, and became more carefree through grieving well, she would enhance her connection to Evie. Samantha knew in her head God was graceful, but she needed to safeguard her heart to keep receiving it.

Like Samantha, we are all prone to trust and default to prideful patterns that make it easy for Satan to bully us. As we begin recognizing and resisting those bully taunts in times of trouble, our heart softens into more of God's grace.

Eight

Encouraging
an Isolated Heart

I find it amazing how the shame of experiencing trials or trouble complicates our ability to receive God's grace. This is especially evident in our tendency toward isolation when we are in distress. Normally, God mediates His grace through the love and support of other people, but during trials we too often turn in on ourselves and away from others in our lives.

The phrase *one another* occurs over a hundred times in the Bible, and more than half of those occurrences provide specific guidance on how to relate to each other. We can so easily forget this counsel in our fallen world, and we pull away from each other when we're hurting. Unfortunately, isolating in affliction make us more susceptible to deception and bullying, which then intensifies isolation—making it harder to reach out for help, and escalating a downward spiral. This hardens and congests our heart, and significantly hinders our ability to receive God's grace.

The Danger of Isolation

Our isolation is what the evil one wants. I cannot tell you how many young couples I've counseled who thought they were the only ones struggling in marriage. The more they felt this, the more they suffered, and the more isolated they became. The difficulty of adjusting to marriage was intensified because they thought they were alone. It's remarkable to watch how a couple will relax when I tell them they seem like a lot of young couples I've counseled who are trying to find their way early in marriage. Just knowing that they aren't alone encourages them, and their hearts soften. I've watched many young couples become part of a small group of couples where they can process the challenges and celebrate the successes of being newly married. That sense of community helps their hearts to soften so they move through initial trials with greater ease.

Isolation is a common and ongoing tactic that the evil one employs to congest our heart and harden us to God's grace. Again, Peter's counsel to persecuted believers provides us with a good reminder to ground our thoughts: "Remember that your family of believers all over the world is going through the same kind of suffering you are." (1 Peter 5:9)

Peter urges those facing persecution to remember fellow believers throughout the world who are also facing trials. He knew that identifying with others who were suffering would help his readers to avoid sliding into a downward spiral.

For grace to move from our head to our heart, we must take seriously the way our heart softens as we nourish the truth that we're not alone in our suffering. If humbly sharing burdens in community were commonplace, it would shape our memories enough so that we would naturally be more responsive to God's grace as we encountered trouble.

Remembering isn't only a rational process. It's not enough to tell ourselves that we aren't alone when life gets hard. We must live that way before the hardship comes, so the reality of it is stored in our heart. Our brain is a social organism that retains memory based on what we feel, how we live, and the nature of our ongoing social connections. If we keep cultivating social support through the ordinary ups and downs of life, it's easier to remember that we are not suffering alone when a more intense trial comes to us.

"Watch out, brothers and sisters, so that there won't be in any of you an evil, unbelieving heart that turns away from the living God. But encourage each other daily, while it is still called today, so that none of you is hardened by sin's deception." (Hebrews 3:12–13 csb) The absence of daily support and encouragement hardens us and makes us vulnerable to deception and sin.

One of the most practical and disarming methods we can deploy to clean out our congested heart is to carry each other's burdens, both large and small, each day. Giving and receiving daily encouragement as a way of life will go a long way in preparing us for trials. We must therefore dismantle walls of denial and pretense that keep our everyday neediness under wraps.

As my wife and I were forming our family, I realized that when I came home and first encountered my wife or daughters at the end of the day, my default question was, "Did you have a good day?" That narrowed their possible responses to "Yes" or "No," and made talking openly about it harder.

To give them opportunities to share whatever was in their hearts, I began to ask, "What kind of day did you have?" This simple step contributed to cultivating an environment that daily invited discussion about difficulties as well as kindnesses.

Walls of Independence

Unfortunately, the vulnerability of living in a fallen world sends us in prideful, self-protective directions, where we can be resistant to regular help and encouragement. As I've discussed, our pride entices us toward behavior patterns that distance and separate us from others, rather than drawing us toward them.

As we grow into adulthood, we try to find ways to avoid the things that bring us pain. One of the most painful wounds I experienced growing up came from the financial fear, chaos, and tension that permeated my home. As in many families, discussing finances was a charged topic for us, one that was best avoided.

I was a "doer," determined to ease the financial tension in our home. I started working in my early teen years to ensure I had the extra money I needed. I had five older siblings, and watching them navigate college expenses helped me decide that I needed to get a college scholarship, so I worked extremely hard at academics and athletics. I wasn't a good enough athlete, nor did I have high-enough SAT scores to earn a scholarship. However, the combination of slightly above-average SAT scores, a high class rank, leadership positions, and extracurricular involvement was strong enough to get me into the Merchant Marine Academy. Landing a free education there accomplished two things at once. I demonstrated that I could take care of myself, and I didn't add to the financial tension in our home. I wasn't just an achiever—I'd now become an overcomer of financial chaos and pain.

I was proud of my accomplishment, and it strengthened my prideful pattern. I didn't recognize how this was moving me away from others. Because my actions were energized by anger at God for the financial chaos He let me endure, it heightened my pride and resentment toward others who had financial ease or blessings they hadn't earned.

In my freshman year at the academy, when I was swabbing decks on Saturday nights, I was simultaneously proud and jealous. I was proud of my ability to do the hard things, and I was jealous of my high school friends who were living in freedom. This internal tension grew over the next four years, and I graduated with a great deal of unrecognized resentment for what I endured to get my "free" education. However, I never questioned whether I should leave the academy, because it was paid for.

After I graduated, I had to work in the merchant marine for five years to pay back the US government for my education. The merchant marine is a high paying industry, so in those years I experienced a newfound financial freedom. I got married halfway through my obligation; and with Dawn and I each working during my remaining years of service, we were able to save a lot of money. But I was too afraid to enjoy any of it. For instance, during that time my wife and I shared a car to save money. I knew I wanted to be in ministry and planned on going to graduate school when I completed my service in the merchant marine. I surmised that having loans on a ministry salary wouldn't be wise, so we saved to pay for graduate school tuition. Although there was wisdom in that direction, I pursued it with fear and self-righteousness that congested my heart toward God and others.

My resentment and fear around finances are the same types of ugly passions we hide in Christian community. During that time, I did not recognize how condescendingly I talked about someone I assumed had an easier way financially. I couldn't see that my financial mindset was in direct contradiction to the clear teaching of Scripture that points us away from financial anxiety and resentment: "Look at the birds. They don't plant or harvest or store food in barns, for your heavenly Father feeds them. And aren't you far more valuable to Him than they are? Can all your worries add a single moment to your life?" (Matthew 6:26–27)

I assented to such biblical truth with my head, but in my heart I lived and breathed like I was on my own financially. My prideful pattern fueled by financial fear became a specific way to lift myself up to be like God. It was a way to deal with wounds (financial chaos), and it blinded me to the knowledge of God. When it came to financial provision, I felt and acted like my own God, and I demonstrated this in my relationships.

I didn't recognize how my prideful pattern was taking me away from God's grace and from "knowing that the same kind of sufferings are being experienced by your fellow believers throughout the world." Those around me suffered other wounds and employed different protective strategies. And I wish I'd been more sensitive to them.

No one goes unscathed in a fallen world, but I couldn't see that well because I was aiming for independence not interdependence. All I could pay attention to were those who had it easier financially, and if I ran into someone who was struggling financially, I focused on ways they didn't work as hard as I did. During that time, I could have moved in the opposite direction and uncovered my wounds, but I followed resentment and fear, which kept me from doing that.

Trials Expose Self-Reliance

The church at Corinth was struggling with self-reliant pride that hinders good community. They thought the Apostle Paul was weak because he didn't use the fancy rhetorical strategies that were respected in their day. Paul believed they misjudged his character, and he suggested that they were proud and were valuing things that nurtured their pride. He used what was going on between them—what they were demonstrating to each other in community—to teach them something about the virtue of humility as seen in Christ, in a culture that has been described as looking down on humility as a weak and feminine trait.

Paul then told them this: "For although we live in the flesh, we do not wage war according to the flesh, since the weapons of our warfare are not of the flesh but are powerful through God for the demolition of strongholds. We demolish arguments and every proud thing that is raised up against the knowledge of God, and we take every thought captive to obey Christ." (2 Corinthians 10:3–5 csb)

The strongholds in our heart—supported by proud arguments—will energize our ego and prevent us from relating with humility. These strongholds are recognized in community, and they are torn down as we follow the Spirit in submission to Christ.

Paul accuses the Corinthians of misjudging his humility because they weren't humble themselves. To foster a more loving community, they would have to uncover the blind spots that were supported by their prideful patterns.

Paul consistently taught that our trials help mold us into the image of Christ and help us develop discerning love. He wrote his letter to enlighten the Corinthians to formational practices he wanted them to employ. He wanted them to recognize how their hard hearts were supported by proud arguments, and how they needed to submit to Christ, to develop more humility, and to demonstrate more love. In fact, he starts his first letter to them with a reminder of how they weren't great people before they met Christ, so there's no reason they should have gotten lost in boasting about themselves. (1 Corinthians 1:26–31) And he later encourages them toward the beauty of other-centered love (13:4–7).

We all need to heed Paul's counsel and foster communities where we allow trials to expose strongholds and proud arguments. Doing this would make it easier for us to remember that "the same kind of sufferings are being experienced by your fellow believers throughout the world."

Being sober-minded and alert against the evil one who bullies us in our vulnerability is never easy; we need each other's help to do it well. Resisting him and staying firm in faith takes courage that needs to be supported by the encouragement of others.

To become believers who are encouraged in moments of affliction, we must form communities that welcome ongoing conversation about sinful beliefs and patterns that are changing slowly. We must stop being surprised by ongoing struggles that fail to evaporate quickly, and which are easier to recognize when we encounter trials. The more we open our struggles to others, and the longer we endure with each other through difficulty, the more our memories will stay grounded in the reality that we all suffer and sin.

I started moving toward my prideful pattern that was energized by financial fear at a young age, and I deepened it with legions of decisions and actions. I thought I was like God and could provide for myself. Trials along the way began to soften that area in my heart, but a hardness built over such a long time cannot come down easily. I needed a significant trial to open my wound more fully and spotlight my need to depend on God and others.

My first position in ministry was as an assistant pastor at a local church in Birmingham, Alabama. We moved there with our ten-month-old daughter and bought our first house. We had our second child within our first year. Three months into our second year of ministry there, I had to go part-time because of financial chaos at the church. I shouldn't have been hired full-time fifteen months earlier. In a season of life when I'd just become more financially responsible than I'd ever dreamed of, I was ushered into the financial stress I'd tried to avoid all my life! My prideful pattern was shattered and inflamed. I vacillated between anger at the church and anger at myself.

I remained part-time at the church for another five years. To supplement my salary, I started a nonprofit counseling organization. The pain and confusion spawned by the whole situation was an excellent opportunity to recognize "strongholds" and "proud arguments" in my heart that I'd been blind to for far too long.

The extraordinary financial stressors at the time helped me see how fear had governed my financial decisions in the past. Even though my degree was in counseling, I hadn't considered working as a counselor because I was too afraid to go out on my own. I wanted the church—or anyone—to "take care of me," because I was nurturing bitterness over having never felt "taken care of" at any point in my life. Even though I indeed had been taken care of in the past, my bitterness obscured those memories.

Because I didn't have time to plan the move toward part-time counseling, I needed help getting it off the ground. One family provided the legal help to set up a corporation and the accounting assistance for taxes and payroll. A team of people donated their time to develop a name, logo, and materials to promote the counseling organization. I hoped to provide counseling for those who couldn't afford it, and I raised funds to make that a reality. Asking for and receiving financial gifts humbled me. My financial unbelief, fear, and resentment were on clear display and were met with help and support. A gaping wound in my soul was being attended to, bandaged, and healed. The proud arguments that congested a hardened heart were being softened.

My resentment toward church leadership was exposing my self-righteousness. How could I keep being angry at mistakes others made unless I thought I myself never made them? I could have asked to review the financial health of the church before I was hired, but I hadn't, simply because I naively believed my hard work and competence would get me through anything. I needed something large to get my attention.

Community Invites Interdependence

For my self-righteousness to be fully exposed, I had to see myself in relationship to others. That's where I recognized covetousness, resentment, and judgment. That—together with the kindness of others—softened me and helped me open more fully to God's grace.

In *Four Models of Counseling in Pastoral Ministry*, Tim Keller writes, "To put it crassly, if we got screwed up in a community, we will be healed only by being immersed in a community that models and provides relationships of truth and love." In the same way, I constructed a proud argument of financial independence in response to being wounded by others, and that argument was torn down through the love of others.

Much of the truth and love I experienced through that trial had been there throughout my life, but the large trial pulled back the curtain of my defenses and helped me see them and respond to grace with more openness. As my prideful pattern was weakened, my heart softened, and I became more responsive. As I endured with others, grace moved from my head to my heart.

After Paul writes about tearing down strongholds and proud arguments in 2 Corinthians 10, he goes on to warn against comparison, suggesting that it's ignorant to use each other as a standard of measurement (10:12). He concludes by declaring that he will "boast only about what has happened within the boundaries of the work God gave him." (10:13)

In a masterful way, Paul affirms several things pertinent to this discussion. Proud arguments have foundations in comparing ourselves to others; they contradict the knowledge of God, keeping us lost in our prideful patterns. My resentment at financial chaos grew as I compared myself to others who seemed to have it easier. I was often propelled to work harder and save more because others seemed to be blessed with financial ease.

We see our passions, strengths, and weaknesses in relation to others. The tension of trials heightens our awareness of these realities, so we feel lusts and hear lies that pull us toward pridefully reasserting ourselves. I was naturally performance-oriented, so it was easy to outdo others, whether it was a good idea or not. I took pride in my "strong work ethic," and I enjoyed flaunting it. I didn't realize I got lost in it.

When I had to go part-time at the church and start a counseling organization to supplement my salary, I was a young father and had more on my plate than I could manage. Because my circumstances made it harder to push myself to get things done, I was naturally invited to take more help, and by God's grace I became more responsive to assistance.

We must fight prideful isolation and move in the opposite direction over time to become interdependent. This begins with believing that the goal of Christian maturity isn't arriving at a point where we don't need others. Instead, God restores our full humanity, including our relational dependence on Him *and* others. He brings out the version of us that He had in mind when He created us, one that's more trusting and less independent.

Christian community shouldn't be a place that pushes us to stand above or apart from others, but instead should nurture the humility to stand with each other. We're strengthened not by a belief in our uniqueness, but in giving and receiving within community. We stand with others because we have strengths that benefit others, and we have weaknesses where we need others.

Consider these words of Paul: "I give each of you this warning: Don't think you are better than you really are. Be honest in your evaluation of yourselves, measuring yourselves by the faith God has given us. Just as our bodies have many parts and each part has a special function, so it is with Christ's body. We are many parts of one body, and we all belong to each other. In His grace, God has given us different gifts for doing certain things well." (Romans 12:3–6)

Paul is encouraging the Romans to think soberly about themselves and to use their strengths for the good of others.

It's humbling to admit and celebrate the fact that someone has a gift we don't have, and to benefit from that. This is reflected in these words from Paul: "Our bodies have many parts, and God has put each part just where He wants it . . . . Yes, there are many parts, but only one body. The eye can never say to the hand, 'I don't need you.' The head can't say to the feet, 'I don't need you.'" (1 Corinthians 12:18–21)

In his writings, Paul discusses human nature with great wisdom. He shows we must push against jealousy and covetousness to support and encourage one another. As we accept, embrace, and demonstrate our differences, we move toward interdependence.

If our sense of self is based on rising above others, we need the pain of falling to welcome God's grace and move toward community with others. If our sense of self is based on posturing ourselves below others, we need the encouragement of others to welcome God's grace and move toward community with others.

Self-Acceptance

Encouragement through community with others leads to self-acceptance, which grows as we're reconciled to God. He chooses how each person is gifted. We bend toward his creative work by accepting our gifting as well as the gifting of others.

Self-acceptance isn't being confident in ourselves or being hard on ourselves; it's being at peace with ourselves. As we grow in self-acceptance, we learn to welcome our strengths as well as our weaknesses, and this posture softens our heart and helps us be more open to God's grace. We need God's grace to accept our own limitations and receive help, just as much as we do to celebrate someone else's strengths while not becoming jealous. When we accept that our strengths and weaknesses are part of who we are, we don't expend energy trying to maximize our strengths or hide our weaknesses in a way that pushes others away from us. Instead, we grow in humility as we stand with others.

A community of individuals marked by self-acceptance will disarm the isolation that comes from following patterns of prideful independence. The softening of self-acceptance invites interdependence as we naturally recognize and play off each other's strengths and weaknesses. In this new dynamic, our hearts are yielding to God's grace through the kind of everyday giving and receiving that ought to characterize Christian community.

I've come a long way from the financial fear and resentment that seemed to own me as a young man. I'm more at rest and more genuinely generous with what God has given me. Pushing through long-held patterns opened my heart to God's grace more than it changed my personality. My bent is still to work hard and be cautious with money, but my heart is more receptive toward God's grace through others, and I know much better that I cannot manage life alone. I still lean on others to pull me away from work or to enjoy what God has given me, just as I help others in their weaknesses.

Pushing through everyday prideful patterns and coming to a place of deeper self-acceptance has strengthened me for times of difficulty. In the vulnerability of trials, it's so much easier to remember that I'm not alone and to refrain from turning in on myself. As I've worked out giving and receiving God's grace in everyday community, it has helped me to find that grace in times of difficulty—because I know more tangibly that the same kind of sufferings are being experienced by my fellow believers throughout the world.

Nine

Refreshing an Exhausted Heart

*O*ne of the first times the fallenness of the world began to impact me (in what may sound like a small example) was when my girls were very young. Something about the sweetness of being together on the weekends made going to work on Monday mornings feel sad for me. I began to realize that I wasn't cut out for being apart from my wife and daughters. I was struck by the realization that the pain of leaving them was a little taste of living in a fallen world.

As C. S. Lewis said in *Mere Christianity*, "If I find in myself desires which nothing in this world can satisfy, the only logical explanation is that I was made for another world." The sadness I felt on Monday mornings was a reminder that I was made for a world without separation or loneliness. In the small but real sadness of those mornings, experiencing God's comfort refreshed me and propelled me toward work with more hope.

As I've suggested often here, the afflictions and trials we encounter can be a training ground to help soften our heart. As we acknowledge the hardships we face and look to God, He provides refreshment to keep us journeying toward heaven.

Having a strong heart doesn't mean we live above the pain in this world; it means our heart has grown the capacity to receive the regular nourishment from God that we need in this world. The Apostle Peter tells us that as we *endure* through trials, God will "restore, support, and strengthen us, and place us on a firm foundation." (1 Peter 5:10)

The process of enduring well through trials helps our heart soften to God's grace on a regular basis. Being on a firm foundation means our heart is less constricted, and we regularly find more life in Christ by yielding to His life in us. On the other side of enduring well, we can proclaim with Paul, "I have been crucified with Christ, and I no longer live, but Christ lives in me. The life I now live in the body, I live by faith in the Son of God, who loved me and gave Himself for me." (Galatians 2:20)

Regularly being nourished by God's grace means we can live more like Jesus in this world. In a lengthy description of the apostles' maturity (in 2 Corinthians 6:3–10), Paul recounts how they're able to "patiently endure troubles and hardships and calamities of every kind." (6:4)

Affliction didn't throw them off course. Toward the end of Paul's description, he wrote of how their hearts were aching, and yet they "always have joy." (6:10)

In that short comment, he describes what's going on in the hearts of the mature. Because afflictions had matured them, the apostles could vulnerably feel sorrow or rejoice at whatever came their way, and their hearts were sustained by God's grace. If they experienced something painful, they could sorrow over it without it pulling them under; if they experienced something delightful, they could celebrate it without believing they'd arrived, and their struggles were ended.

In a fallen world, soft hearts stay nourished by grace through sorrowing and rejoicing. The apostles experienced the up-and-down nature of a life with tribulations and triumphs, and they grew into a robust faithfulness supported through sorrowing and celebrating.

Surrendering to Compassion

Jesus was a man full of grace who walked through this world with unmatched maturity. Surprisingly, His maturity wasn't characterized by a lack of sorrow or heartache. He's described as being "despised and rejected, a man of sorrows, acquainted with deepest grief. We turned our backs on Him and looked the other way. He was despised, and we did not care." (Isaiah 53:3)

The relationships Jesus experienced in this world were the opposite of what He was used to. *We turned our backs on Him, we despised Him, and we did not care.* Even though His life was full of relational rejection, Jesus stayed refreshed in a fallen world by turning toward the Father in sorrow.

It's hard for us as human beings to fully comprehend how beautifully the Father, Son, and Holy Spirit relate. They completely understand each other, love each other, and work together in effortless ways. There's no jealousy, pride, or manipulation. That's one reason God is described as an affectionate and tender mother and father in the Scriptures (as in Luke 13:34 and Psalm 103:13). We can picture what God is like by watching a parent tenderly care for their child.

As a divine human being, Jesus accessed God's tenderness through tears. "While Jesus was here on earth, He offered prayers and pleadings, with a loud cry and tears, to the One who could rescue Him from death." (Hebrews 5:7)

Jesus's tears sustained Him in this world because His sorrow connected Him with the Father's heart. Out of His own experience, Jesus taught, "God blesses those who mourn, for they will be comforted." (Matthew 5:4)

Through His tears, He was refreshed by the Father's comfort.

Like Jesus, we're supported in a fallen world by communing with God through our sorrow. *Humility* is the willingness to receive God's compassion. *Lamenting* is experiencing God's compassion through confusion, doubt, and anger. *Groaning* is connecting with God's compassion amid pain. *Interdependence* is giving and receiving that compassion in human community. *Sorrowing* is vulnerably surrendering to that compassion as a way of life. By that surrender, we declare, "God's tenderness and care will keep me refreshed in a fallen world."

As our heart is softened through trials, we mature into sorrowing well, in an ongoing way. We can practice and posture ourselves toward sorrowing well, but only over time—as our heart becomes less congested—can we vulnerably sorrow as the need arises. As we then encounter fallenness in this world, we become like Jesus—"a man acquainted with grief."

For the first twenty-nine years of my life, I ran away or hid from sorrow. It would sneak out of me occasionally, but mostly I focused on picking up and moving ahead. Then I began my training as a counselor. I was confronted with how congested my heart was, and how much

I suppressed my emotions. I fought against this exposure, but slowly it crept closer to my heart.

During that training, Dawn and I experienced a bout with infertility before we had our first child. One morning I was having coffee with a friend, and I let him know that Dawn was pregnant again (this was our third pregnancy in less than a year, with the first two ending in miscarriage). After I revealed this news to him, he began to engage me in further conversation about the pending pregnancy.

My friend knew that experiencing infertility with my young wife had been difficult for me. He kept asking me questions to expose my hope, which I was pushing down because I feared we would experience another miscarriage. After some time of thoughtful discussion, he said, "I think you're a better man than to live without hope!"

His words were working on me as I walked to the car after our time together. Sitting inside my car, I prayed these words: "Okay, Lord, I'm going to hope with all my heart that this pregnancy leads to a baby, and if we miscarry again, I'm going to grieve with all my heart. Either way, I want to live like You are alive."

Although the Holy Spirit had been moving me toward such a moment, it was brought more clearly to my consciousness by a friend. He helped me cast my lot with the Lord, regardless of what affliction might come.

My wife experienced the loss from our miscarriages more fully than I did. Her sorrow scared me, and I wanted to run from her too. By God's grace, I had friends who encouraged me to move toward her in the loss she experienced. The process of caring for someone I loved, and trying to feel what she felt, had a transforming impact on me. Her tears were softening the hardness of my heart. It was easier to feel her sorrow than my own, and it helped me work backward toward mine. During that time, I experienced more lamenting (*God, why are you doing this?*) and groaning (*God, I can't take this anymore*), but occasionally I sorrowed (*Hold me, God; I need you*) through my fear and pain.

After I graduated from the counseling program, I started working at a residential treatment center for adolescents who'd been removed from their homes because they had either been abused or were abusing others. As I met with those adolescents and their families, I wanted to demonstrate incarnational love, like Jesus. I didn't want to relate to them from a safe distance.

One of my first counselees was a fourteen-year-old girl who'd been sexually abused by her grandfather. As she told me her story, I listened and wept. Several days later, she said to me, "I never knew that what happened to me was sad until I saw your tears."

That was the first time I remember my sorrow being affirmed, and the first time I realized a soft heart was a good thing.

While working with those teenagers and their families, I was regularly confronted with emotions I'd spent a lifetime suppressing. There were weekends when I told my wife I needed to watch a sad movie to help me feel and grieve the sorrow I'd encountered through the week. During those years and beyond, I was developing emotional muscles I'd never even exercised.

Somewhere in the middle of that time, my wife and I watched a movie together that painted a picture of a young boy who felt like an alien in his world. I connected with his story. Five minutes into the movie, I began to cry profusely and continued to weep through the whole movie. I wept and wept and wept.

As my wife and I walked to the car afterward, I told her, "I've been sad my whole life, and pretended I wasn't. I can't do it anymore."

Refreshment in Sorrow

My own passage into sorrow may help you picture what refreshment in sorrow looks like. Christian growth is more like farming than manufacturing. We till the soil, fertilize, plant, water, weed, and wait . . . and wait . . . and wait.

Months later, something surprising pops out of the ground.

We can study and read about sorrowing, but most of all we must stay attentive to the life in front of us, praying, seeking, and yielding to the Lord toward change. I was confronted with the hardness in my heart and my refusal to sorrow. I had to accept that the hardness was real; I had to lament, resist, groan, and pray my way into a softer heart and more secure connection with the Lord.

Eventually, I began to sorrow losses as a way of life. They no longer stored up in my body and weighed me down. They no longer prompted the intensity of questions or fears that created disorientation toward God. I grew more able to meet others in their sorrow and share it with them. As I recounted earlier, when my brother died by suicide (which occurred seventeen years after I grieved our first miscarriage), I was able to grieve through it and remain encouraged by God's grace. My heart had softened and was regularly more receptive, so I was refreshed with grace even as I grieved his death and the brokenness it uncovered in my world.

My practice at grieving through the years was like training for a big race, and it prepared me to go the distance in the face of a much larger loss. As I processed my brother's death with those close to me, the grief felt like everyday conversation that moved toward connection and peace, whereas the grief of the miscarriages seventeen years earlier felt like walking through quicksand.

Although sorrowing our first miscarriage wasn't a loss as grave as my brother's suicide, it felt darker and harder. I did more lamenting and groaning through the earlier loss. The miscarriage was the first time I moved toward sorrowing, and I didn't have the emotional and spiritual muscles to do it well. I had to push through condemnation from the evil one toward God's tenderness. Years later I moved through a larger loss with more refreshment, because I was more surrendered to God's compassion and could receive it in an ongoing way.

We must recognize grieving as a mature and necessary part of maintaining strength to navigate a fallen world. It's an everyday means for God's grace to move from our head to our heart. "Sorrow is better than laughter, for sadness has a refining influence on us." (Ecclesiastes 7:3)

Sorrowing well changes us, because in moments of sorrow we surrender to God and say, "Hold me. Comfort me. Heal me. This world is too big and hard for me to navigate without Your help."

As our heart softens, God's grace pours in. Sorrowing is like a water stop on a marathon run. It refreshes us to stay in the race.

"What joy for those whose strength comes from the Lord, who have set their minds on a pilgrimage to Jerusalem. When they walk through the Valley of Weeping, it will become a place of refreshing springs. The autumn rains will clothe it with blessings. They will continue to grow stronger, and each of them will appear before God in Jerusalem." (Psalm 84:5–7)

For those on a pilgrimage—aliens and foreigners navigating a fallen world—sorrowing is a place of refreshment. It strengthens us on our way to meet the Lord.

Types of Sorrow

There are three different kinds of sorrow that meet us in a fallen world.

The first type, *anguish*, comes as we experience evil in this world. This kind of grief acknowledges that Satan is the prince of this world, and becomes a prayer for God to nourish and energize us as foreigners and aliens so we can continue to navigate this world with His love. Such sorrow is mixed with anger because it recognizes evil.

Jesus felt anguish before he raised his friend Lazarus from the dead. (John 11:33–35) Entering the grief of Lazarus' family brought Jesus' anger and sorrow to the surface. He was angry that they had to suffer, and He was sad that they were hurting. So, He wept with them. His sadness helped Him connect with His friends, and His anger propelled Him to action. In raising Lazarus from the dead, Jesus was proclaiming that suffering in this world will not have the last word. For a moment He pushed back evil. When Lazarus walked out of the tomb, He foreshadowed a coming resurrection that would change everything.

We feel anguish when we encounter evil because we're in touch with our desire to push against it. It's a reminder that sin, suffering, and loss are not our friends. We must recognize them as realities in this world, and sorrowing helps us do that. But as we hold onto anger, it energizes us to keep moving toward justice and to participate in building the coming kingdom. Often a person in these situations will experience *only* anger, or else *only* sorrow. If we feel only anger at injustice, we become bitter and resentful, and if we feel only sorrow, we become weak and passive. Anguish is a mixture of sorrow and anger that fosters strength to keep moving against injustice in this world.

The next type of sorrow is *contrition*. We experience this after we have participated in evil or otherwise advanced evil—we've fallen prey to the evil one's deception and persecution, and followed his ways in opposition to God. In contrition, we recognize how we cooperated with evil and made choices that conspired against God's goodness. David felt contrition when he said, "I recognize my rebellion; it haunts me day and night. Against You, and You alone, have I sinned; I have done what is evil in Your sight." (Psalm 51:3–4)

Contrition helps us experience God's mercy in our sin. Remember, we don't grieve like people who have no hope (1 Thessalonians 4:13). In worldly sorrow, we beat ourselves up about sin, leading to despair and curving in on ourselves. Worldly sorrow leads to death (2 Corinthians 7:10). In redemptive sorrow, we remember that we don't want to sin, and that sin will one day be gone. Grieving our sin becomes a vulnerable prayer, asking the Lord for help in glorifying Him.

Paul says his flesh buffeted him in such a way that he did things he didn't want to do, and failed to do the things he wanted to do (Romans 7:18–19). He concludes, "But if I do what I don't want to do, I am not really the one doing wrong; it is sin living in me that does it." (7:20)

Paul doesn't take personal responsibility for his sin in the way we often think about it. Nor does he despair in it. He demonstrates sorrow over his sin, while also recognizing that he's battling forces bigger than himself. His vulnerability—his recognition that sin is bigger than his choices alone—opens the door for God's grace to minister to him in his contrition. In contrition, we vulnerably turn toward the Lord for Him to heal and refresh us, so we can do what He wants us to. "For the kind of sorrow God wants us to experience leads us away from sin and results in salvation. There's no regret for that kind of sorrow." (2 Corinthians 7:10)

The last type of sorrow is *yearning*. This sorrow tells the truth about how God brings good out of bad. It acknowledges His sovereignty and coming kingdom. It's a wistful, hopeful type of sorrow laced with pain. It's letting the hope of redemption lift us up.

One of the first times I remember consciously experiencing this kind of yearning was a passing moment at dinner. My oldest daughter was about five years old and had spilled her milk. She didn't flinch or become afraid. She said, "I made an accident."

Seconds later, I began to sob. Her response pierced something in my heart. As a young father, I was fearfully hoping and working to build a family where my daughter felt safe and known and didn't cower when she experienced a mishap. The fact that she didn't fall apart at spilling her milk suggested that this was becoming a reality. I heard the Lord saying, "You're already in that family you're striving to build. Stop working so hard and enjoy it a little. I won't forget you."

I didn't realize how afraid and alone I felt being a father. My sorrow in that moment was a hopeful surrender to God's goodness, receiving the truth that He'd been with me all along, and nothing could separate me from His love.

The yearning in this sorrow recognizes that the kingdom is coming, and we experience tastes of it here on earth that simultaneously help us to wait for it and long for it. We remember that all will be set right, and our present tears help us connect with God, Who's already there in the future. They refresh our hope and endurance and help us participate more fully in building God's kingdom.

Sorrow Moves Us Out of Ourselves

Each type of sorrow pulls us out of ourselves. Anguish nudges us toward justice. Contrition draws us toward mercy. And yearning supports enduring faith.

As our heart is softened and refreshed through sorrow, we more passionately give and receive grace with others, which enhances our experience of God's kindness in this world. Our ability to love and do what is good is energized from inside.

Humans are two parts—inner and outer. Our inner person (thoughts, emotions, longings, and choices) determines what we do with our outer person (our mouth, ears, eyes, hands, arms, and legs). What we do grows out of who we are. Sorrow moves us to act like God because it's a vulnerable invitation for Him to pour His grace into our inner being, our soul: "God blesses those who mourn, for they will be comforted." (Matthew 5:4)

Sorrowing refreshes and enlarges our compassion, and compassion energizes loving demonstrations of the Gospel. Compassion is not just feeling; it's a form of love that produces action to alleviate suffering. The Gospel accounts record Jesus feeling compassion as He healed (Mark 14:14), fed (Matthew 15:32), taught (Mark 6:34), and loved (Matthew 9:36–38). Jesus demonstrated what God is like.

Like Jesus, as we accept the difficulty of living in a fallen world and learn to sorrow, we look to God for refreshment. Sorrowing is a bridge toward deeper dependence on the Lord. It helps us come alive with Christlike compassion so the grace we received from the Lord turns us outward, toward others. In sorrowing well, we're refreshed to live the Gospel. Grace moves from our head to our heart, and compassionately compels us to become more like Christ to others in our world.

Ten

Strengthening a Feeble Heart

*C*an you imagine what it will be like when God establishes His kingdom in fullness here on earth? "He will wipe every tear from their eyes, and there will be no more death or sorrow or crying or pain. All these things are gone forever." (Revelation 21:4)

No more death, or sorrow, or crying, or pain. That will be a glorious day—enjoying God and the beauty of who He is and all He does, without any troubles. What a celebration! Although we can imagine that day, we still live in the "now and not yet." God has established His kingdom on earth, but it's under attack. We're moving toward heaven, but we don't experience it in fullness.

The Vulnerability of Joy

Cultivating joy is vulnerable because it comes and goes. To experience the bliss of heaven one moment and the torments of hell the next can make it seem like we're not in our right mind. Experiencing beauty for a moment, while knowing that future pain will come, makes fostering joy a daunting journey. Our fleshly mind will whisper, *If I can't be in control of joy in my life, then I don't want or need it. Better not to live with the heartache of it coming and going.*

Because we cannot control joy, many of us turn inward toward manufactured joy. In *A Long Obedience in the Same Direction*, Eugene Peterson says, "A common but futile strategy for achieving joy is trying to eliminate things that hurt; get rid of pain by numbing the nerve ends, get rid of insecurity by eliminating risks, get rid of disappointment by depersonalizing your relationships. And then try to lighten the boredom of such a life by buying joy in the form of vacations and entertainment. But that kind of joy never penetrates our lives, never changes our basic constitution."

Trying to manufacture and be in control of joy will congest our heart and make receiving joy more difficult.

Instead we must learn to willingly hold joy and pain together. The paradox of welcoming joy as a gift we cannot control begins with accepting the fact that we cannot avoid pain. Hearts that welcome affliction are more connected to this reality about God: "He knows how weak we are; He remembers we are only dust." (Psalm 103:14)

Clearly we can't escape heartache here in this world, and we need God's help. In addition, accepting the fallenness of this world helps flush out our inner deposits of resentment, bitterness, or rejection. As we turn toward the Lord while we grieve through trials that expose our fear, unbelief, and sin, He cleans out our congested heart, and we become more grateful. Then we see joyful experiences as appetizers—smaller tastes of heaven—that rejuvenate us and help us wait for the full-course meal.

Joy is the most vulnerable emotion in our heart, and is welcomed best when we've been softened and strengthened through affliction. "Those who plant in tears will harvest with shouts of joy. They weep as they go to plant their seed, but they sing as they return with the harvest." (Psalm 126:5–6)

As we endure through the consequences of living in a fallen world, and we vulnerably welcome and nurture joy, it strengthens our feeble heart. By enduring, we're saying, "God has not forgotten us," and our heart is strengthened to build and wait for the coming kingdom. It's a vulnerable act of courage and defiance in a world under siege. In *Understanding People*, Larry Crabb says, "Joy is distinctly an eschatological thing—it is rooted in the future. Joy now is not to replace suffering and pain, it is to support us through it."

The Fight to Remember

We begin cultivating joy by remembering. Our fleshly nature is a magnet for such emotions as fear or despair, and it will hold onto whatever reinforces those emotions and repel whatever fosters joy. Therefore, we need to attach more fully to the good we experience. That's why we need celebrations like a graduation party. It's why we need to tell and retell stories of surprisingly good or fun moments. The good in our lives too easily falls to the background of our mind and becomes hard to access.

Take for instance a moment many years ago when I got home from work and started wrestling and playing with my three young girls. They were cackling and smiling with great delight. As I took in the expressions on their faces, I was struck with how much they were enjoying me and our time together. The Holy Spirit prompted me: "Why don't you remember these times and connect to them? Why do you find yourself more regularly harboring thoughts of your weakness or sin as a father?"

At that moment I realized that even my memory was corrupted by my sinful nature. I experienced many joyful moments with my girls from day to day, but I wasn't remembering them. Instead, I gave in to frequent temptations to nurture painful memories and failures that left me despondent. I marginalized joy-filled memories that would contribute to buoyant hope. Instead, we must remember joyful moments we've experienced.

Our memories serve a purpose, because they tell a story. When we are passive and naïve, our memories will get swept up by the evil in this world and tell stories that detach us from God and His caring involvement in our life.

Two commands we find repeated throughout the Scriptures are to remember and to rejoice. Our fleshly tendency is to forget and despair. The fathering memories I held onto told the story of an absent God and a mean father. I talked and obsessed more about my parenting mistakes than about recollections that would bring me hope.

As our heart matures, we grow inwardly stronger by remembering and embracing joy-filled moments. Neuropsychologist Rick Hanson has popularized the science behind this reality. In his book, *Hardwiring*

Happiness, he describes how our brain is like Velcro for negative experiences and Teflon for positive ones. It will automatically attach to what is negative and repel what is positive. We must dwell on what's positive for at least fifteen to twenty seconds for our brain to attach to it. To be regularly strengthened in God's grace through joy, we must work to attach to it through remembering, and this takes effort. "Fix your thoughts on what is true, and honorable, and right, and pure, and lovely, and admirable. Think about things that are excellent and worthy of praise." (Philippians 4:8)

It would be natural to assume joy would be easier than sadness, but it isn't.

I've found that clinging to beauty and goodness is especially difficult and necessary in long-term relationships, as with friends, coworkers, or family. My wife and I inevitably wounded each other regularly in the first half of our marriage. As we slowly grew into more mature forms of love, we were still plagued with memories of past pain. To participate in God's coming kingdom and to celebrate His grace and work in our lives, we had to confront memories of past pain that often showed up as resentment.

In *Forgive for Love*, Fred Luskin notes, "The common tendency is to feel that your experience of hurt is more real than your ability to love. It is important to challenge this belief and also to challenge the very human tendency to say that the painful experiences your spouse causes go deeper than the love you feel for them."

As I remembered and attached to joyful and redemptive moments, they solidified, and I stood up in them. It gave me strength to live like God had not forgotten me. I had to confront resentment to do this, but it was worth it.

Consider how Moses spoke with the Israelites after they were released from bondage: "Just remember what the Lord your God did to Pharaoh and to all the land of Egypt. Remember the great terrors the Lord your God sent against them. You saw it all with your own eyes! And remember the miraculous signs and wonders, and the strong hand and powerful arm with which He brought you out of Egypt. The Lord your God will use this same power against all the people you fear." (Deuteronomy 7:18–19)

Remember, remember, remember . . . so that as you approach the next frightening or painful situation you recognize His presence with you, and His willingness to act for you. In speaking to Israel at that moment, Moses reminded them to actively remember the mercies of God we witness with our own eyes, because our tendency is to forget. And when we forget that God has done good things on our behalf, we lose our hope-filled joy in His fierce and faithful love.

As we retain memories of joy, we're more attuned to God's goodness, and we look for His grace. It strengthens our faith and helps us reject the lies that say God doesn't care about us. As a result, His grace more readily moves from our head to our heart, and helps us enter the ongoing joy of kingdom living.

Forgetful Joy

In addition to remembering the joy-filled moments in our lives, we must practice forgetful joy. To endure the pain of a fallen world, we need to hold onto good moments (remembering joy) and experience daily kindness in a way that can be called forgetful joy.

If we were training to become elite athletes, we would make room for moments of rest, and get massages or whirlpool baths, and make sure we ate nourishing food. We wouldn't feel guilty for soothing and attending to aches and pains in our body—it would make sense. In fact, not doing so would be negligent. Our spiritual life is no different. If we do the hard work of welcoming difficulty and letting it work on us, we must make room for moments that help us rest and forget the pain. This is forgetful joy.

Forgetful joy is an experience of delight that comes from partaking in God's creation and celebrating physical reminders of our eternal home in Heaven. This helps us bear up under the ongoing affliction we experience as foreigners in a strange land ruled by the accuser. Forgetful joy evolves from the simple pleasures God provides to help disarm the pain of a fallen world.

Forgetful joy comes to us each day. It can be a good night's sleep, a cup of coffee in the morning, a relaxing lunch, a good book, or a humorous exchange with a friend. Forgetful joy is making room for and partaking in the sensuous pleasures God gives each day. We're human beings in a fallen world, living with deteriorating bodies in time and space. God knows this, and He uses His creation to mediate His grace to us.

Worship involves celebrating the Creator by enjoying His creation. After the Israelites returned from exile, there came a day (as told about in Nehemiah 8) when they gathered in a public square in Jerusalem, and the law of God was read aloud to them. The people were overcome with sadness because they hadn't honored this law. Nehemiah, their governor, wanted them to remember that God's grace was real to them that day, and they could celebrate it. He said to the people, "Go and eat what is rich, drink what is sweet, and send portions to those who have nothing prepared, since today is holy to our Lord. Do not grieve, because the joy of the Lord is your strength." (Nehemiah 8:10 csb)

He wanted His people to enjoy God's gifts and be strengthened.

As I began to recognize this with greater clarity, my mealtime prayers shifted more to this: "God, all the good in my life comes as a gift from You. Eating is a helpful reminder that You're kind and provide for me. This meal helps massage out the pain that has found its way into my heart today. As I partake, help me rejoice in Your goodness."

If we're attentive and receptive, the simple gifts of this life connect us with the Lord's kindness and help us forget the weight of this fallen world. "Naming" this type of joy means embracing it as a gift from the Lord's hand and turning away from our tendency to make it an idol. The more we grow in God-consciousness of the daily goodness He brings our way, the more each one of His gifts leads us into worshipful joy.

In my college days, I drove I-80 across Pennsylvania one autumn day to visit my sister. It's hard to miss the splendor of fall colors on this route. Many people are enraptured by this beauty as they weave through those rolling hills. But as a young college student, I wasn't impressed. When I got back to campus on Long Island, I was thinking, "What's the big deal with the fall colors? Why do people take long weekends just to drive out to Pennsylvania to see them?"

Decades later, I was driving down I-65 in Alabama during the fall. I looked out my window and was struck by the beauty of the fall colors. I prayed inwardly, *Thank you, Lord.* I experienced the beauty of God's creation as a gift that brought joy to me. Gratefulness flowed out of my heart because a lifetime of trials had transformed me from a self-satisfied college student into an attentive man with a heart softened to receive God's goodness. It had always been true that God's invisible qualities could be witnessed through nature (as we're told in Romans 1:18). It is still true that "the heavens proclaim the glory of God" and "the skies display His craftsmanship." (Psalm 91:1)

But to humble my heart enough to appreciate and celebrate this truth, it took enduring well through difficulty over time. Being humbled by hardships helped me not only to be stunned by creation; it helped me also to connect with the Creator.

I knew something in my late forties that I didn't know in my twenties: I couldn't overcome this world in my own strength, and I needed help and encouragement from the Lord to make it day by day. I was therefore more open to see His gifts, receive them, and celebrate them with joy and gratitude. God had been pursuing me with His kindness for a lifetime. However, I had too much "me-consciousness" to recognize this. As I was humbled, God's grace (which had always been near me) found its way from my head to my heart. More and more I received daily pleasures in this life as gifts from a Friend who knew I needed them, and they helped me taste His kingdom and wait for its full coming.

Connected Joy

Another type of joy is one that we can call connected joy. It goes deeper than forgetful joy because it goes beyond the sensuousness of physical pleasure and touches us in the depths of our soul. Connected joy is deep contentment from experiencing an intimate touch from the Lord, a touch that reminds us He hasn't forgotten us, and that we'll one day see Him face to face. It's a joy that David acknowledged before the Lord: "You will show me the way of life, granting me the joy of Your presence and the pleasures of living with You forever." (Psalm 16:11)

In connected joy, we understand more clearly how much God intimately cares for us. For instance, when a kind friend calls us to encourage us in a difficulty, this will impact us differently than taking a warm bath. They both bring us enjoyment in the moment and can arouse thankfulness to the Lord, but the phone call—because of its relational dynamic, goes deeper. In fact, if the person making the call knows us intimately, the joy stirred by their words will penetrate deeper and bring us closer to the Lord.

Frequently, believers look for connected joy only through prayer, meditating on Scripture, or gathering with other believers in specific acts of fellowship or worship. These are undoubtedly primary conduits of connected joy. They are ways we can experience intimacy with God, but practicing them over time softens us to the point where we more readily experience God reaching out to us through a different means—through our difficulties in life.

Whenever God uniquely uses one of the many avenues under His authority—friends, a sunset, music, food, good movies and books—to personally care for us, we experience connected joy. As we soften and mature during a trial, something like a beautiful sunset might penetrate our heart and encourage us in a way it wouldn't have years before. It helps us remember that God hasn't forgotten us, that He sees us, and that He's reaching out to us in our difficulty to help us endure. As our God-consciousness grows, it keeps our countenance lifted toward the Lord and makes it harder to totally get lost in despair or discouragement.

Connected joy also happens as we endure with others through difficulty. You may have had a friend who was struggling in his vocational life. You saw how much he disliked his job, and you knew he had the ability to find something else. You walked him through his fears and roadblocks and encouraged him at every step. Several years later, after he'd switched vocations and experienced trying times at the new job, your friend receives a promotion. In that moment, it's abundantly clear that the job change was a wise decision. You're getting a drink with that friend to celebrate their promotion, and as you reminisce, it occurs to your friend how much you were a part of his journey. As your friend puts words to that reality, you both experience connected joy. God's grace carried you both toward that moment, and you're grateful to Him and for each other.

One day we'll see God face to face. On that day, joy will permeate us fully, and we'll rest completely in the unfettered beauty and bliss of His presence. Between now and then, God is reconciling us to himself and will reach out to communicate His specific love to our heart. As we attach to Him or others in those moments, we experience connected joy.

I'm hoping that each of us—if we stop and think—could practice at remembering joy and recalling moments of forgetful joy and connected joy. It's important to celebrate the grace of God that our joy-filled moments represent. Letting the joy of the Lord seep into our heart strengthens our inner feebleness by reinforcing hope. We may believe God is good in our head, but cultivating joy as a gift helps that reality take residence in our heart.

God is already in His kingdom, and He's waiting for us to be with Him in fullness. Jesus endured the scorn and shame of the cross for the joy that was on the other side. As we enter that now, we're experiencing the joy of the kingdom He instituted. The joy of the Lord is our strength. Celebrating His goodness with regularity strengthens us, as His grace moves from head to heart.

Eleven

Reminders for
an Unsettled Heart

*F*or now, the fallenness of the world partially blocks and distorts our knowledge of God. But it has never hindered His perfect knowledge of us. "All that I know now is partial and incomplete, but then I will know everything completely, just as God now knows me completely." (1 Corinthians 13:12)

In those words, can you hear Paul's yearning for the God to whom he's fully exposed? There's no hint of cringing or shrinking from God's gaze.

If we could experience being fully known by God, the extent of His kindness toward us would not be in question. As His grace fills our heart completely, the fear that unsettles us would be gone. We would be fully at rest. "Perfect love expels all fear. If we are afraid, it is for fear of punishment, and this shows that we have not fully experienced His perfect love." (1 John 4:18)

We long to know our security in God's love. In the meantime, we keep moving toward a fuller experience of it.

I could end this book with a call to action or a passionate plea for us to implement the ideas I've articulated, in hopes that it would get us there quicker. However, when it comes to our relationship with God, we're responders and not initiators, and yielding to Him is the swiftest way forward. Forced effort won't speed up the process of grace moving from our head to our heart. However, increased vulnerability and trust will make the path more seamless.

For moving more fluidly along the path of change, a prayer like this will help: "God, I don't believe I'm the source of my change. *You* are. I ask that You help me cultivate the truths I've read about, and please keep reminding me of them as I encounter affliction."

It's best to walk by faith while seeing the Christian life as an ongoing journey—one in which trials strip off our chosen fig leaves, and God stands ready to meet us in our nakedness, longing to clothe us with His grace. To some degree we never reach the journey's end in this life, and we have to become willing to keep following the Lord into more. Even the Apostle Paul said he hadn't reached perfection, but he kept moving forward to garner more of the love God first reached out to give him (Philippians 3:12–14).

Enduring well through difficulties involves increased responsiveness in which we allow His divine compassion to encounter the parts of ourselves that have cringed away from Him. Whenever we receive His gaze, His love dissolves our fear. In this way, ongoing trials invite us to experience ourselves as more fully known by God, so that we can receive more rest for our unsettled heart during life's pain.

As we walk that journey, several reminders will help us.

The Journey Is Slow

God promises a lot up front, and He delivers slowly. It takes time to get used to His pace.

We see this played out in God's relationship with Abraham. God began this relationship by arousing Abraham's desire through grand promises: "I will make you into a great nation. I will bless you and make you famous, and you will be a blessing to others." (Genesis 12:2)

But God didn't tangibly move forward in fulfilling this promise until a quarter-century later, with the birth of Abraham's son, Isaac. That pace is representative of how God works. "You must not forget, dear friends, that a day is like a thousand years to the Lord, and a thousand years is like a day." (2 Peter 3:8)

In the time it took to experience the realization of the promise, Abraham developed trust in God as he wrestled with Him about his desire for a son. Meanwhile there were many moments when Abraham doubted and questioned God through the process of being more known by Him.

Our own journey toward friendship with God and finding security in His grace is no different. We'll wrestle with Him over issues in the here and now (like wanting a new job or desiring a child), and through hindrances along the way that bring doubt or despair. God will often seem like an uncaring friend. His intentions are hard to trust during our trials because evil tempts us to doubt them.

When I started counseling, I thought the biggest questions I'd help people answer were, "Why am I here?" and "Where am I going?" I've been surprised to find that instead, most people instead are asking, "Why's it taking so long?" or "How come it's so difficult?" The pain people experience over unmet desires makes waiting extraordinarily difficult.

In *Objects of His Affections*, Scotty Smith notes, "Interestingly enough, the most asked question in the whole Bible—from Genesis to Revelation—is 'How long, O Lord, how long?' And the most repeated command from God is 'Do not fear' or 'Do not be afraid.' The people of God consistently cry out for relief, and the God of love bids us trust Him."

As waiting challenges our heart, our sinful nature will pull and prod us to trust ourselves. God knows that our battle with control and selfishness makes it hard to live by faith. He also knows that the surest way to transform these fleshly tendencies is to receive His grace with an open and vulnerable heart. As God's steadfast love seeps in, it helps soften the pain and disappointment we have experienced along the way. It helps us transfer our allegiance from the objects we love (including ourselves) to the God who cares.

If our trials resolved themselves quickly, we wouldn't attach to God in any lasting way. His slow pace invites our heart to stay open, looking outside ourselves for His comfort. It builds settled trust as we receive His love over a longer period. God's pace is designed to build the qualities He values—humility and trust.

Jesus used several metaphors to describe the coming kingdom and why the religious leaders were missing it. He said, "What is the Kingdom of God like? How can I illustrate it? It is like a tiny mustard seed planted in a garden; it grows and becomes a tree, and the birds come and find shelter among its branches." (Luke 13:18–19)

Jesus spoke this parable right after healing a woman on the Sabbath, which had enraged the leaders of the synagogue. His intention was to continue exposing the religious leaders' pride. Religion for them was a source of power and recognition. They therefore expected the Messiah to bring more of the same, and to quickly and powerfully establish His (and their) rule on earth. Jesus's kingdom conflicted with the Pharisees' goals, so they failed to recognize it. Through this metaphor of the mustard seed, Jesus gave them an opportunity to understand their misguided notions. The kingdom grows in ways that require humility and trust, not power and control. Kingdom growth always starts small and slowly increases in size. When Jesus said the kingdom of God grows like a tiny mustard seed, He was using a popular colloquialism that His listeners would understand; "as small as a mustard seed" meant as small as possible, since hardly anything was smaller.

Although we long for the "whole tree" of resting in God's grace, it will never start with more than a mustard seed, and it will be nurtured along the way with small doses. We need not be surprised when we're aiming toward something large, while in the moment we have very little. In moments when we're straining for more, we'll be tempted to think, *That little ounce of grace or rest or trust we feel from time to time will never get us where we want to go.* But the truth is that an ounce is all we need.

Anyone who has grown to the place where they're more regularly comforted by God's grace has started each new part of their journey with only a tiny seed of trust. Our anxiety over having only a mustard seed of trust is just like a builder being anxious he wouldn't complete a house when all he could see was the foundation.

As we long for grace to move from our head to our heart, and to be at rest in our friendship with God, we must stand up to mocking whispers that we don't have enough to work with, or that we'll never get there. Even if we've made progress and are displaying new character or experiencing more of God's grace, the evil one wants to obscure it. The growth process requires celebrating small victories. "Do not despise these small beginnings," said the prophet Zechariah, "for the Lord rejoices to see the work begin." (4:10)

For example, I may have been counseling someone for several weeks when I notice a small change. I'll take a moment and affirm this. Usually the person will say something like, "That's no big deal," or, "Anybody can do that." I'll keep talking about it, and I help them accept it. As I encourage them to trust God more and to celebrate this small victory, they'll usually be a little unnerved. Trusting God feels uncomfortable, and we have to battle evil's mocking voice to grow into it. So I'll help them accept the awkwardness of trust and its place in the life of the Christian. Over time, as God's love and grace seeps into our heart, we trust His friendship more and accept His slow pace.

The Irony of Christian Maturity

As our hearts are softening and we're maturing, things can seem like they're getting worse.

Early in my Christian journey, I thought maturity meant I would feel good about myself and confident about life, and that I would come through perfectly in every circumstance. In my pride, I was aiming toward independence instead of aiming to depend on God and His grace. I didn't think maturity meant increased interdependence—more reliance on grace from the Lord and others as an everyday reality. Instead of giving me perfect confidence in every situation, stronger faith has meant moving more restfully into situations with needs beyond my resources and questions beyond my answers. I have only a vague sense that I'm doing good and that it will matter, and I wait on the Lord for the outcome.

Those periods of waiting inevitably expose areas of sin and unbelief. As I've kept growing more secure in God's grace, I've seen my sin and lack of love more clearly. In times past, recognizing this would have owned me and caused me to shut down. Now I can move forward using the breastplate of righteousness as my defense. This armor is a gift of grace to shield me in my weakness and nakedness; it's not an accomplishment of my own strength.

I don't love others perfectly, and I can't. As the evil one condemns me for areas of sin that expose my weak love, I hold up the breastplate of righteousness and continue to move toward others imperfectly, covered by a grace that's not my own. I don't love others because I've arrived; I pursue it as a God-given privilege that comes through Christ's righteousness in me. Even though that involvement shines light on nuances of sin I didn't see when I was on the sidelines, God's grace now "sneaks" into my softened heart and holds me, so that I'm able to keep loving others while grieving where my love falls short.

God cares for us tenderly and will support us faithfully, but He wants to be on an adventure with us in which we learn to trust in darkness and to dare greatly despite hardship. That's what friendship with Him involves. Softened hearts, regularly filled with grace, navigate forward with more courage. They long more deeply, see more clearly, and live more maturely.

Such a posture is different from our early seasons as a Christian, because in the beginning we need to soak in God's nurturing and protection. It's similar to the way an infant depends on his or her parents. However, to mature in faith we cannot stay infants. Our faith must be tried and tested to mature.

I remember a transitional part of my journey where it seemed I was regularly in over my head. I felt like Paul when he wrote these words: "You ought to know, dear brothers and sisters, about the trouble we went through . . . . We were crushed and overwhelmed beyond our ability to endure, and we thought we would never live through it. In fact, we expected to die. But as a result, we stopped relying on ourselves and learned to rely only on God, Who raises the dead." (2 Corinthians 1:8–9)

On a regular basis, I found myself in situations that were more and more challenging. It seemed like God stopped caring about me. I couldn't see that being more filled with God's grace helped me step out into situations and stay involved, when previously I would have retreated out of fear. I felt like a kid who left home for his first semester of college, full of homesickness. I was scared and nervous about growing up, and I wanted to go back to safety.

During that transition, I moved away from a heavy dependence on "Christian" activity (Bible studies, prayer meetings, reading Christian books, etc.) that marked my faith in the beginning, and I began to live life and taste Jesus more through the way I involved myself with others. The Holy Spirit was guiding me out of self-absorption. He was saying, "Go live life. Stop hiding behind religious duty. Perhaps as you meaningfully engage with others, and give yourself away, you'll want to talk to Me and investigate My word because you'll need to, and all those verses you've memorized will begin to penetrate your heart and mean more to you!"

Along the path toward maturity, I had to keep realizing that there was no going back to the comfort of immaturity. The "safe" start to my Christian life was for the purpose of forming me into a person who gave his life away. As I gave up what seemed like a close relationship with the Lord to become more engaged with the world—to face harder questions, and to hurt more with others—it seemed like things were getting worse.

Those who stay in the newborn stage of faith maintain a heightened focus on comfort or blessing, which only fosters self-absorption and pride. In that stance, struggles often get blamed on sin or a lack of knowledge, instead of being recognized as necessary obstacles to help us deepen trust and gain wisdom. Maturity often involves becoming comfortable with feelings of incompetence, experiencing more pain, and caring for others in a way that leaves us feeling that God is more distant. If grace is transforming us to live like Christ in this world, then we see the brokenness of this world more plainly and feel the pain in this world more deeply. This propels us toward needing more grace, not less, to stay involved. We therefore have to exercise into softer hearts that are gradually able to open wider and take in more of God's grace.

As we mature, we begin to adapt to this process of having our heart stretched. God will invite us into situations we aren't adequate for, and this won't surprise us as much as it used to. We'll know—better than we once did—that trials are not pass or fail, and that nothing strange is happening to us. Instead, like all who ever hoped in the promises of God, we're being refined in our faith. "This makes it clear that our great power is from God, not from ourselves. Through suffering, our bodies continue to share in the death of Jesus so that the life of Jesus may also be seen in our bodies." (2 Corinthians 4:7,10)

One of God's most common responses to the troubles we encounter is not alleviating them but supporting us through them. As we're stretched into more of ourselves and fit into them, we live out the Gospel with more fullness. In our head we know truths like, "It is better to give than to receive," (Acts 20:35) and "Those who refresh others will themselves be refreshed." (Proverbs 11:25) But to live these out from our heart, we must become more mature through difficulties.

Somewhere along my journey, my heart softened enough that God's grace more readily poured into my heart and helped me wait for more of it. I could move through challenges and fears that seemed to indicate I was going backward. As I matured, I started recognizing many of the trials I faced were not a result of my failure, but were passages into greater Christlikeness and increased fruit.

Our Peace with God Is Real

We are God's children, and He is at peace with us. That's not a subjective statement.

After explaining justification by faith early in the Epistle to the Romans, Paul turns his attention to the path of maturity for the Christian, beginning with these words: "Therefore, since we have been made right in God's sight by faith, we have peace with God because of what Jesus Christ our Lord has done for us. Because of our faith, Christ has brought us into this place of undeserved privilege where we now stand." (Romans 5:1–2)

We're at peace with God, and we're able to stand up in that peace by the grace we've received through faith.

It's a journey to stand that way and to experience the peace with Him. We must keep refocusing the eyes of our heart as we experience trouble in this world. Notice the personal pronouns in these verses: "In *His* kindness God called you to share in *His* eternal glory by means of Christ Jesus. So after you have suffered a little while, *He* will restore, support, and strengthen you, and *He* will place you on a firm foundation. All power to *Him* forever! Amen." (1 Peter 5:10–11)

His, *He*, and *Him*. Trials strip away our self-protection and invite the possibility of strengthened intimacy with God, as we open to His grace. They help us practice at being vulnerable with God so we can welcome the comfort of His love.

I invite you to consider ways to do this and to foster deepened intimacy with God. It's often hard to keep remembering that God is at peace with us, because trials and troubles naturally arouse doubts about God even as they open us up to experience His help. As fears and idols are exposed through trials; and as we receive God's grace more deeply, our sense of peace with Him can increase. Over time, the reality of our friendship with Him becomes more secure.

Trials cause periods of haziness for any human, and can make faith seem hard to grasp. In such times it's important to remember that our feelings don't determine our standing before God. Phillip Yancey says, "Faith means trusting in advance what will only make sense in reverse."

This is unequivocally true when our heart becomes unsettled by trials. Evil will use difficulty to sabotage our peace with Him, raising doubts about God's love and commitment toward us. So I pray that another voice gets louder and louder through the years. That voice says, "I'm at peace with you, but you're filled with sinful flesh and are pressed by a world that will lie to you about My love for you. You need to endure things that will cause you to question Me, and in those vulnerable moments—as I hold and comfort you—you'll take ownership of how much I care about you. You're not alienated from Me. We're at peace with one another, and you're on your way to be home with Me forever."

Our peace with God is realized most profoundly in contexts that make Him seem most distant. Trials that feel like the withdrawal of His care actually help us experience the *His*, *He*, and *Him* of God's grace. When we speak of this grace, it's not as though we mean to say grace is one face of God that He can choose in the moment to wear or not. No, God's attention to us *always* flows from His unchanging character. In our trials, God—who is love itself—speaks to the fears and wounds we experience. The paradox of enduring through trials is that they slowly bring our doubts and fears into the open for God to speak to them and soothe them in profound ways.

Remaining open to God through trials does something inside us that fills our heart and lifts our countenance toward Heaven. As our heart is softened and God's grace flows into us more freely, we begin to taste fully the reality of Heaven on earth, and it settles us.

We were made to be at peace with God, and because He has accomplished that peace and is always graciously disposed toward us in Christ, our experience of peace with Him grows as we endure well through affliction. The journey is slow, and things often seem to be getting worse as they're getting better, but we're at peace with God.

May His grace move from our head to our heart, so we experience more of it while we wait to see Him face to face.

"There is wonderful joy ahead, even though you must endure many trials for a little while. These trials will show that your faith is genuine. It is being tested as fire tests and purifies gold—though your faith is far more precious than mere gold. So when your faith remains strong through many trials, it will bring you much praise and glory and honor on the day when Jesus Christ is revealed to the whole world." (1 Peter 1:6–7)

Resources

Allender, Dan B. and Tremper Longman, *Cry of the Soul: How Our Emotions Reveal Our Deepest Questions about God* (Colorado Springs: NavPress, 1994).

Crabb, Larry. *Understanding People* (Grand Rapids, Michigan: Zondervan, 1987).

Hanson, Rick. *Hardwiring Happiness* (New York: Harmony, 2013).

Keller, Tim. *Four Models of Counseling in Pastoral Ministry* (Gospel in Life. Retrieved from http://www.gospelinlife.com/four-models-of-counseling-in-pastoral-ministry, May 12, 2010).

Lewis, C. S. *Mere Christianity* (New York: Harper Collins, 1952); and *The Problem of Pain* (New York: Collier, 1962).

Luskin, Fred. *Forgive for Love: The Missing Ingredient for a Healthy and Lasting Relationship* (New York: Harper Collins, 2007).

Peterson, Eugene. *A Long Obedience in the Same Direction* (Downers Grove, Illinois: Inter-Varsity, 1979).

Powlison, David. *Power Encounters: Reclaiming Spiritual Warfare* (Grand Rapids, Michigan: Baker, 1995).

Smith, James K. A. *You Are What You Love: The Spiritual Power of Habit* (Grand Rapids, Michigan: Brazos, 2016).

Smith, Scotty. *Objects of His Affections: Coming Alive to the Compelling Love of God* (Brentwood, Tennessee: Howard, 2001).

Thompson, Marjorie. *Soul Feast: An Invitation to the Christian Spiritual Life* (Louisville, Kentucky: Westminster John Knox, 1995).

Wolff, Pierre. *May I Hate God?* (New York: Paulist, 1966).

Yancey, Philip. *Disappointment with God: Three Questions No One Asks Aloud* (Grand Rapids, Michigan: Zondervan, 1988).

Acknowledgments

My sincere thanks to all who have supported and assisted me in the process of writing *Grace from Head to Heart*. Each passing year I become more grateful for the training I received under Dr Larry Crabb and Dr. Dan Allender. Their influence continues to run through everything I write and speak. I'm grateful to Dr. William Clough for starting me on a journey toward a richer and more nuanced understanding of trauma.

One of my greatest joys is being an adjunct professor at Beeson Divinity School where I get to interact with and mentor so many thoughtful students. They help to shape my understanding of God's grace. Several past and present students assisted with my thinking in this book; my thanks to Michael Davis, Ryan Martin, Ryan Linkous, Rachel Wood, Corey White, Laura Henrich, Mitchel McEver, and Ethan and Kadie Smith.

My friends Jodi MacNeal and Ellen Padgett provided significant help in the formation of this book, and long ago Julie Sparkman suggested the title. I am grateful for their assistance.

Heartfelt thanks to my wife Dawn and our daughters: Aimee, Abigail, and Elise. You are immeasurable doses of God's grace each day, for which I am profoundly grateful.

About the Author

Before Gordon C. Bals became a teacher and pastoral counselor for the last twenty-five-plus years, he graduated from the United States Merchant Marine Academy and worked on oil tankers and tugboats. He has a master's degree in Biblical Counseling and a Doctor of Education in Pastoral Community Counseling.

He first served as an adolescent and family therapist and then as assistant pastor at a local church in Alabama. He is the founder and director of Daymark Pastoral Counseling, a nonprofit organization that has provided counseling and teaching for more than two decades that is designed to help others experience restoration with God and those they love. He has been an adjunct professor for twenty-plus years, the last decade at Beeson Divinity School in Birmingham, Alabama, where he teaches pastoral counseling classes.

Dr. Bals is the author, with Jodi MacNeal, of *Common Ground: Discovering God's Redemption in Your Marriage*. He is a sought-after counselor, teacher, and seminar leader who helps people understand the intersection between God, the important relationships in their life, and the "Good News" of the Gospel.

The depth of love and life he has experienced as the husband of Dawn (since 1990), and father of Aimee, Abigail, and Elise, have richly informed his writing and teaching. He is originally from the Jersey Shore but has resided in Birmingham, Alabama, for most of his adult life. In his free time, he likes to be outdoors, reading a book, eating good food, and spending time with family and friends.

Made in USA - North Chelmsford, MA
1301168_9780988328327
01.31.2022 1645